Vital Vintage Church

How Traditional Congregations Thrive

Rev. Michael S. Piazza

Dedication

To Bill Eure and David Plunkett who moved halfway across the country with me because they believed that, together, we could renew a Vintage Church that almost everyone else had given up on. Although it was harder than we thought, a church thrives today because we took a chance and gave it our best. I never could have done anything without the two of them being the real wizards behind the curtain.

Contents

Acknowledgements

If it is true that we are products of our experiences then I am a product of church and churches. I fell in love with church when I was eight years old, and I never left. I was licensed to preach in the United Methodist Church when I was only 18. Growing up, all I ever wanted to be was a Methodist preacher in South Georgia, but, when I met my partner in 1980, the Methodists decided I was unfit for ministry. Fortunately, the Metropolitan Community Church didn't agree, so they gave me a home. In a very real sense, I owe them my life. The Methodists taught me to expect to spend four to six years with a church, but, as it turned out, the Cathedral of Hope spent more time raising me than my parents did. In my 22 years with them, I learned a lot about church, about myself, and about life and death. To walk with that faith community through the season of AIDS will always be the greatest honor of my life. Through that church I met the United Church of Christ and set out on the great adventure of working with congregations that date back to the founding of the country and are ready to be made new.

It has been a wonderful life thanks to all of the churches I have loved who were willing to love me to this place:

- Statesboro First United Methodist Church; Statesboro, Georgia
- The Cochran Circuit: Antioch, Longstreet, Friendship United Methodist Churches; Cochran, Georgia
- Lake Park United Methodist Church; Lake Park, Georgia
- Lake United Methodist Church; Tulsa, Oklahoma
- Haygood Memorial United Methodist Church; Atlanta, Georgia
- The Greater Atlanta Metropolitan Community Church; Atlanta, Georgia
- St. Luke's Metropolitan Community Church; Jacksonville, Florida
- The Cathedral of Hope-United Church of Christ; Dallas, Texas
- Virginia-Highland Church; Atlanta, Georgia

Each of these churches taught me so much and endured me learning from so many mistakes. What an amazing honor to have lived and loved and learned with you. Thank you for letting me share on the following pages a little of what you taught me.

Introduction
Invigorated Vintage Churches

I often take my daughters shopping when they come home from college. I have helped them pick out their clothes throughout their entire lives. There was a period while they were teenagers, however, that I lost my touch completely. They hated anything I thought was cute, and I was embarrassed by the things they liked. Then, suddenly, everything changed. Our tastes found common ground. What is strange now is where they want to shop. Fortunately for me, they never have had expensive taste, but now they want to go to Goodwill and other places that sell used clothing. I've tried to explain that I actually can afford new clothes for them, but they complain that most stores at the mall don't sell the clothes they want. For them, and for most of their friends, everything old is new, and cool, again.

In my computer bag I have a telephone handset that looks like one from the old black rotary phone my grandmother used. It is designed, however, to plug into my cellphone. A woman told me after a recent talk I gave that her eight-year-old grandson was always using the words "vintage" and "retro." Finally, she asked him what he meant by those words. He said, "Oh, it is all this old stuff that is really cool." Perhaps you've noticed the cultural revival and love affair with things that are retro, so why hasn't the church?

For more than 40 years, since becoming a student pastor at the age of 18, in four states, and 14 congregations, I have been a part of growing churches. From three new church starts, to churches so old they lacked indoor plumbing, from a progressive Southern mega-church, to a moribund liberal Baptist church, it has been my experience that churches can grow without abandoning tradition, liturgy, vestments, hymns, ritual, or sacraments. Yes, mainline churches are declining, but it isn't because of their worship style or values. The congregation I currently pastor quadrupled in attendance in just a couple of years. This happened in a traditional redbrick building with a white steeple that looks like a Baptist church your grandmother might have attended. The clergy wear albs and stoles, and we sing hymns accompanied by an old pipe organ. Every week, we read at least two passages from the Bible, and we serve communion. Seventy percent of the congregation is new, and almost 100 percent of them are under the age of 40. They are married and single; people of color and white; lesbian, gay, bisexual, transgender, and heterosexual; professional and blue collar. They are reclaiming Vintage Church with great passion and enthusiasm. Most of the new people who have been coming say that the liturgy and tradition are two of the things they love best.

So, what is the difference for this old church? Why is this Vintage Church growing, while most mainline churches with the same customs and characteristics are declining? It might be possible to dismiss this as an anomaly, but it has happened too often in too many different settings not to pay attention to the dynamics that have caused this growth and are causing other traditional churches to grow in unlikely settings. Through the years, when the churches I have served have grown, some media accounts have credited my leadership, preaching, or charisma. While that is flattering, it is simply not true, and that is not false modesty, I assure you. I have lived long enough and worked with enough churches to know what is and is not true. I do have gifts and talents, but they are not extraordinary. I work very hard, but many of my colleagues are much more industrious and productive. There are moments of creativity, but most are adapted or appropriated from others who are far more inventive. What we have done so successfully can be replicated by those who love the church as much as I do.

In the following pages we will look for clues together. Dr. Fred Craddock, who taught me preaching, loved to say, "Good preaching is not so much speaking *to* people as it is speaking *for* people." What he meant is it may be a sign of good preaching when someone responds to a sermon having heard what you *did not* say. As a preacher, my job is much more to evoke insights and awareness than to impart them. My hope is that, in the chapters ahead, you will find yourself nodding because it is an affirmation of what you have suspected all along. It also will be a success if you reject the ideas that I suggest in favor of the creativity that bubbles to the surface in you.

The purpose of this book isn't to tell you what we have done and compel you to do it, too. My goal is to stir you to your own insights. You are the expert for your setting, not me. Trust your own wisdom, but always keep in mind that if we keep on doing what we have always done we will keep on getting what we've always gotten. That hasn't worked out so well in most churches.

Chapter One
Contextual Despair

The mainline church is dying.

Isn't that how books like this one are supposed to start? The trouble is I don't believe it. Oh, even I cannot deny that mainline churches are declining and that some denominations do not have a long life expectancy. Aging, shrinking, and decline, however, are not the same as death. To paraphrase Aragorn's speech from the movie version of J.R.R. Tolkien's *Lord of the Rings*:

> *My brothers and sisters, I see in your eyes the same fear that would take the heart of me! A day may come when the courage of humans fail, when we forsake our friends and break all bonds of fellowship. But it is not this day. An hour of wolves and shattered shields when the age of humanity comes crashing down! But it is not this day! This day we fight! By all that you hold dear on this good Earth, I bid you stand people of the West!*

The day may come when the traditional mainline church that we know and love dies, but it is not this day … at least it does not have to be. All of the churches the Apostle Paul founded around the eastern Mediterranean are gone, so it certainly is true that, like every other living organism, churches have a life cycle that includes an ending point. Let me suggest, though, that our existential despair about the church is, to some extent, feeding the decline and creating a self-fulfilling prophecy.

To be brutally honest, all too many of my colleagues have lost hope for the future and are holding on until retirement. I had a pastor explain to me how he had calculated the rate of his church's decline and knew that it would last long enough for him not to need to move before retiring. Therefore, he was not going to make challenging changes that might offend one or two large donors, even if it might give his church "a future with hope."

All too many of our church leaders have become caretakers and hospice chaplains presiding over the final days of a dying institution. That very attitude and energy have deprived the church of new ideas, creativity, and the inestimable power of hope. Yes, the traditional church is going to have to retool and largely reinvent itself. Yes, the Spirit seems to be raising up new expressions and those experiments should be encouraged, supported, and given every opportunity to flourish. Yes, we live in a world where variety is the norm and "one size fits *some*." None of this is sufficient cause, however, to pronounce last rites over the traditional church.

Perhaps we would benefit from setting the church's decline in a historical context. Let's begin with some boring but enlightening statistics. First, people seem to attend church much less often than they think. Researchers call this the "halo effect" because Americans tend to over report activities like exercise, volunteering, church attendance, giving, and voting, but underreport things like speeding, drinking, and viewing pornography. This halo effect not only gives us inaccurate statistics, but it has a significant effect on the average attendance and giving in the local church. People are not as active and faithful as they think.

This was reflected in a recent conversation with a young (20-something) couple in the church I pastor. The young man, who serves on an important committee, expressed chagrin when I said that we had missed them. He explained that since they bought their new house they have been spending time remodeling it. "I know we haven't been in several weeks, but we'll be back," he said lightly. The truth is that, as I write this, they have not attended church in more than eight months. He may not keep track of these things, but I do.

Like every organization that relies on attendance for its support, the church has suffered a significant decline in the past two decades. Membership has remained strong, and giving has even been reasonably healthy in many places. There is generally positive regard for most local churches, even though esteem for church in general has fallen. People simply are not attending worship as often, and they apparently aren't even coming as often as they think they do. When a person's "regular attendance" drops from twice a month to once a month overall Sunday attendance declines by half. Much of what has been interpreted as the "death of the church" is nothing more than a reflection of the struggle all attendance-based institutions are facing. There are some things that can help, but an accurate diagnosis is necessary to determine the right prescription. We also must find alternative ways to evaluate the health of our churches other than only the number of warm bodies in pews on Sunday mornings.

Unfortunately, older folks who love the church and are there every Sunday are dying off, and the generation that has followed simply isn't going to be present in your pews as often. It is more a reflection of the pace of their lives than of how they feel about the church, or about your church. Even older members are living busier and busier lives and are not present with the consistency they once were. The one member of our church that I can count on being present almost every Sunday is in her 90s. Most of her family and friends have died, so it is critical to her that she be present every week to connect with people she loves and who love her. God bless her; the church will sorely miss her generation of faithfulness. It will not be seen in our pews again.

For many years American pollsters reported that 40 percent of Americans attended church every week. These numbers were consistent in survey after survey. Then, as more and more churches began to use computers to track and report attendance, demographers like C. Kirk Hadaway and Penny Long Marler began to report very different figures. In 2005, in *The Journal for the Scientific Study of Religion*, Hadaway and Marler revealed that the actual number of people worshipping each week is closer to 17.7 percent—52 million instead of the formerly reported 132 million. In other words, part of the decline in attendance is not that people don't like church as much, but that we now have more accurate numbers.

Church historian Martin Marty has also tried to remind us of the dangers of nostalgia:

> *Colonial America was not as church-bound and church-moved as [author David Aikman] suggests. He*

does better with the 19th century, when religious prac-
tice did take hold not only among Catholic newcomers
but also revived Protestants. So how were things in the
good old days? A consensus questioned by a few seri-
ous scholars—Patricia Bonomi among them—is that
fewer than 20 percent of the colonial citizens were ac-
tive in churches. Change came after 1776, so that, in
one common estimate, church participation jumped
from 17 percent to 34 percent between 1776 and 1850.
A better past, more illuminating for comparison in
present concerns, is between the early 1960s, when
participation crested, and today. (www.eth-
icsdaily.com/church-attendance-wasnt-always-
robust-in-past-cms-20169)

In short, if you are reading this, it is highly likely that the overwhelming majority of your church life has been spent in an anomalous historic church-attendance bubble. In the wake of World War II people began to attend church with increasing frequency, and this continued through the baby boom of the 1960s and even into the early '70s when the current decline began. What we have been internalizing as the death of the mainline church and the decline of the Christian faith may be assessed more accurately as a return to a more normative state. Yes, that means that a smaller percentage of people attend church now than in the 1950s and '60s, and, yes, much of that attendance shifted from the mainline to evangelical and nondenominational churches, and, yes, that will mean some congregations will die. I believe, however, that we may be nearing a point of stabilization, and there may even be cause for optimism.

The other historical anomaly that has greatly impacted the mainline church is the way the role of women in society has changed since World War II. That has become a cliché, but one aspect of this oft-repeated truism that has rarely been examined is how that changing role specifically impacted the vitality of the church and the bubble it created.

During World War II several hundred thousand women served in combat roles, and, by 1945, more than 2.2 million women were working in the defense industry. Countless other women took over running stores, farms, and workshops, while more than 15 million young American men went to war. Men and women faced a change in roles and identity that was forced upon them by the global conflict.

When the war was over, the women who served in the military were expected to return to their homes. The men came back and, by and large, claimed the jobs that had been filled by women, who also were expected to return home. While that may sound simple and obvious, hundreds of thousands of women had been changed by their experiences and found being a homemaker insufficiently challenging. They had developed new skills, discovered new gifts, and uncovered a confidence in their own capacity to do more than keep a good home. What they had discovered was that, unlike men, they could keep the house *and* change the world. Many of these women went to the institution they knew best outside their homes: the church. There, they did much more than volunteer. They went to work, essentially, as unpaid staff. They started ministries, programs, mission organizations, and served as volunteer staff and leaders for booming congregations.

My friend and colleague Rev. Mary Lee-Clark observed that, in the wake of the war, families returned to church in gratitude, seeking stability and normalcy. The post-war baby boom motivated parents to fill the pews and take their children to Sunday school. Thousands of women found outlets for their newly-honed leadership skills, and husbands who feared they might never have a family were more than happy to sit in the pews of churches where the pastor or priest was usually a man, but where almost all the other jobs were performed by competent women.

While much has been written about the societal changes that the 1960s brought and their contribution to the decline of the mainline church, nothing was more responsible for that decline than the fact that women were entering the workforce more and more often. Young women went to the office rather than to the church as their mothers had. Flush with an influx of money from these new double-income households, churches often expanded their staff to replace this loss of female leadership. That expanded staff masked church decline for a time but could not forestall the inevitable loss of energy, leadership, attendance, and giving.

This shift was followed in short order by the rapid growth of the evangelical church. This more socially conservative theology and social approach to faith attracted people shaken by the rapid transitions of the '60s. Evangelical churches grew rapidly, particularly in the South and suburban America where mostly whites fled to escape city schools and racial integration. Today, the decline of the more mainstream Baptist churches seems to be determined to mirror the decline of mainline churches before them. By a savvy and aggressive use of media, the conservative church gave the impression that it was a larger portion of American Christianity than it actually was at the time. Of more import, they also gave the impression that they were the norm for the church, and successfully marginalized and, in some cases, even demonized the mainline church. This public redefining of Christianity attracted people away from the traditional churches, and, more importantly, it made those who might be attracted naturally feel the church really wasn't for them. We allowed Christianity and the church to be redefined without ever offering an alternative narrative.

None of this is to say that the mainline church is not declining; rather, lest we continue to respond in the wrong ways, it is to put it into some context other than what has been offered most frequently. Misdiagnosis leads to erroneous remedies. In my own United Church of Christ (UCC), the explanation too often offered, even by my progressive colleagues, is that, because of our Northeastern roots, the UCC is more liberal than most Americans. The irony is that the values expressed in many progressive churches today are quite congruent with younger people and those who now are participating in the reverse migration from the suburbs back into the city. What we offer as an excuse for our decline actually could identify our greatest potential opportunity for attraction and renewal.

Urban hipsters, newly-formed families, and empty nesters who are choosing the diversity of the city eschew the thinly-veiled racism and overt nationalism offered in too many flag-waving churches. Most of these folk will not attend churches that do not welcome their gay and lesbian family and friends. They are looking for places that treat the earth and creation as sacred and something to be preserved and protected. Diverse community is how they believe life is meant to be. Their values are our values, though, in many settings, one must ask, "How would they know that?"

It is not that the mainline church is "too liberal"; rather, it is too tepid. We have been so afraid to alienate the older, more conservative members who pay our bills that we have failed completely to create strategies for inviting those who find the values of our community congruent and compelling. This "either/or" approach has rendered us impotent for long enough. The church must find the resources and resolve to both love and nourish those who decreasingly fill our pews and, at the same time, appeal to those who could fill them for the future. What we cannot afford to do is serve only the needs of a constituency that is dying while neglecting the fastest growing portion of the population that checks "none" when asked about their religious preference.

If we can see the decline of our churches in a different historical context we might let go of our morbid obsession that we are dying and that this fate is imminent and inevitable. Yes, if we keep doing what we always have done we WILL keep getting the same, poor results. However, if we can find new ways of being church to the spiritually hungry millions who share our values, we might discover that Vintage Church is just what they are looking for. Perhaps they never even knew it because we apparently didn't know it either.

Chapter Two
Liberating Your Church

If you can forgive the lifetime habits of a preacher, I'd like to offer two stories from scripture that describe how to begin the process of reviving a Vintage Church. In Matthew 12:9-14, Mark 3:1-6, and Luke 6:6-11 you find the miracle story in which Jesus heals a man with a "withered hand." It is probably told in all of the Synoptic Gospels because Jesus got in trouble for the healing. This was one of those times when he defied the traditional religious understanding of observing the Sabbath laws and healed anyway. Perhaps what also caught the writers' attention was the miracle took place in the synagogue. I suspect, like our churches today, that was one of the last places people expected God to show up and work a miracle.

According to Matthew, Jesus seemed to know that people were just looking for a reason to accuse him, so he addressed his critics before he acted:

> *Jesus said to them, "If any of you has a sheep and it falls into a pit on the Sabbath, will you not take hold of it and lift it out? How much more valuable is a man than a sheep! Therefore it is lawful to do good on the Sabbath." Then he said to the man, "Stretch out your*

hand." So he stretched it out and it was completely re-stored, just as sound as the other.

I suppose addressing our critics proactively might be one of the principles for congregational transformation, but that wasn't what got my attention in this story. Although it is unclear what malady the man in the story suffered, a "withered hand" might be an apt description of the state of many mainline churches. It isn't that we are missing a limb. Rather, we have found our hand shrunken in power and usefulness, and we have lost power and flexibility.

Notice that Jesus does not magically create a new hand and then attach it to this man's wrist. In fact, there is no indication that Jesus touched him or did anything for him other than simply tell him to stretch out his hand. It was the man who did the work in response to the call of Jesus. Suddenly, perhaps miraculously, it seemed the whole and healthy hand, which had been within him all along, was called forth by his confidence to respond to the authoritative call of Jesus.

Now, like any biblical parable, it is risky to press this too far and, even more perilous, to artificially apply it to another subject. However, Jesus courageously confronts standard religious assumptions, sees new possibilities through eyes of mercy and compassion, and calls forth the health and strength and wholeness that, of course, is God's ultimate dream for us all. Let the church hear what the Spirit is saying.

As I have worked with churches around the country, I have seen this miracle repeated time and again. Oh, there are times when an old church needs to die and a completely new church needs to be born, and there are times when the vegetable garden of something very new needs to be planted in the fading flower garden whose season has passed, but there also are many times when what has too long been dormant simply needs permission to become alive and strong and functional again. We need to hear the call of God to stretch out of our withered state and move into healthy functioning. We don't need a new church; we need a REnewed church.

On occasion, I have been in a restaurant and wanted something that was different from what was described on the menu. The server or cashier often will respond by saying that they don't have what I want. If I can resist the urge to remind them that I am the customer, I can sometimes gently suggest that, by doing something quite simple, they can provide what I need or really want. Almost always all that was needed was for someone to give them permission to see the possibilities and do something differently. It is amazing how powerfully that also works in churches. We often poke fun at ourselves by saying our most sacred phrase is, "We've never done it that way before," or "But we've always done it that way." It is my suspicion, though, that the church simply is waiting for someone to give them permission to try something new or to challenge them to do some old things in new ways. Almost everyone I know loves to hear old musical favorites played to new rhythms and beats. Who knows? We might even decide to learn some entirely new tunes ... but I don't want to get carried away.

In his book *The Proper Bostonian*, Cleveland Amory tells how John Lowell ate oatmeal for breakfast every day for 50 years. Then, one morning, his wife burned the oatmeal, and there was no more. When his wife told him that, tragically, there would be no oatmeal for him that morning, John Lowell responded, "That's alright, my dear; I never really cared for the stuff anyway."

That seems to describe the way many churches go through life. We live oatmeal lives: bland and unsatisfying, routine and mundane, assuming that everyone else must be enjoying it. The church cooks oatmeal every Sunday morning, appealing to the lowest common denominator when a divine purpose burns before us, beckoning our souls. Disciples of Jesus are called to live lives of splendor and glory. No oatmeal for us; it is jalapenos with Tabasco from now to the finale!

It is remarkable how many churches are willing to try something new but never have had the chance. One grumpy congregant has paralyzed many a church whose only hope is that the naysayer dies before the church does. As a guest preacher and consultant, I often have said things in sermons or workshops that apparently were challenging enough to cause people to gasp. When I turn to see, it is all too often the pastor or leaders who were shocked. The people in the pews were far more open to hearing the challenge and stretching into their dreams. They almost always know that something new is needed and have been waiting and, I suspect, praying for someone to come along and call forth the new life that already is present within them. What I love about being a consultant is the opportunity not to create life, but to be a midwife for the life that is waiting to be born.

The other biblical text we might consider as we seek to call forth the vibrant, vital, healthy church within is found only in John. It is such a startling story that none of the Synoptics dared to tell it. In John 11, we find the long story about Jesus raising Lazarus from the dead. If healing on the Sabbath, and in the synagogue no less, got Jesus into hot water, raising the dead may have been what got him killed.

This is a familiar story, but I'd like to focus on one component. It is a parable about Jesus' power over death. We are called to believe that even death recoils at Jesus' command and Lazarus thus comes to life again. What always calls to my soul in this miracle story is how, when Lazarus came forth from the tomb, he was still bound up in grave clothes. Again, this seems an apt picture of the mainline church today. Even when life seems to break out around us and threatens to bring us out of our tombs, we still insist on shuffling about bound up in grave clothes. Even the smell of death lingers in too many old sanctuaries. (Would it kill us to buy air freshener?)

In this parable, we are reminded that, although only Jesus has the power of resurrection, our role as Jesus' servants is to strip off the grave clothes so the dance of new life can begin. I'm not sure an entire book like this one can come up with a better job description for pastors and leaders who are seeking to revive the church we love. You and I do not have the spiritual power to resurrect a church that is dead; however, again and again, I have seen courageous leaders set loose a church that is alive, but moribund in tradition, structure, conflict, confusion, despair, and hopelessness.

No, the mainline church will not return to its glory days of the 1950s and '60s, nor should it. What we must do is unleash the amazing life-giving power of grace, forgiveness, restoration, community, devotion, hope, purpose, and meaning that always has been the mission of the church. In our malaise and despair, we have turned our energy inward, focusing on institutional survival. Nothing could have accelerated our decline more. The institution as we have known it doesn't have to survive, but the mission and ministry of God's transforming love and grace must. In order for that to happen, the church may have to take new forms and find new expressions. We most certainly will have to release our current way of living from the grave clothes we have mistaken for an Easter dress.

Meetings must give way to ministry. Structures must become more agile and permission-giving. We must celebrate experiments that fail because they move us closer to what is needed. New songs must be learned, and old favorites must find new tempos and tunes. Spiritual practices must be reclaimed and practiced in newly invigorated ways. Vintage church may look like something from the past, but it must function like something for the future.

I suppose Lazarus must have been the same person when he came out of the grave, but, if that story is true on any level, Lazarus never could have lived the same life. I have recounted, on many Easters, the story found in a 1925 play by Eugene O'Neill. "Lazarus Laughed" is the story of the post-resurrection Lazarus. O'Neill seemed to think that the primary characteristic that described the risen and liberated Lazarus was laughter. In the play's first scene, Lazarus' father gives a banquet, and people around the table are casting glances at Lazarus and whispering, "He looks different, doesn't he?"

Someone else says, "There is nothing about him that's like it used to be. You remember how Lazarus used to be? He was so dull and insipid, the least desirable member of his family. But look at him now. Positive. Confident. Decisive. And listen to him laugh."

"It seems like," another says, "all Lazarus does is just laugh and laugh and laugh."

In the play, Lazarus goes about telling others what has happened to him and who is responsible for the effusive joy of his new life. He is eventually arrested for his passionate and persistent witness to faith. I can't help but believe that the real reason they bothered with him was the power of his effusive joy. He is taken before the Roman Emperor Caligula, who says to him, "If you do not stop what you are doing I will have you killed." And Lazarus laughed, and he laughed, and he laughed, and he laughed, until one of the characters in the play says, "His laughter was like wine, it made my whole soul drunk."

The mainline church has been given up for dead. I hope I am not the only one laughing at that. I hope that you will join me and that we will laugh and laugh until we make the souls of the entire world drunk. I do not know exactly what the future holds for us, but, as disciples of the great Resurrector, our job is to set people free to live again. We might start by letting the Spirit call forth the life that is in our own churches and stripping off the grave clothes so they might live again. At a recent wedding I watched as a grandmother who had hobbled into the room suddenly began to dance. It was likely the dance of her own wedding or the other joyful celebrations she had known that brought her to her feet. Soon, though, she was alive in the moment and shone brighter than the bride because she gave hope and joy to all of us.

Chapter Three
Bringing Worship into the 20ᵗʰ Century
(I'm not asking for a miracle!)

After being at the Cathedral of Hope UCC for 22 years, I began working as a consultant helping to renew mainline churches. The first thing I had to do was discover if I still knew anything relevant that would grow a church in the 21ˢᵗ century. Every church I had ever served had grown, and none more than the Cathedral of Hope, which grew from a couple hundred members to more than 4,000. The general fund budget grew from $280,000 to more than $4.5 million, and weekly attendance went from 280 to 2,200. No one was more amazed or mystified than me.

That story is great, but people want to know how. More importantly, they want to know if what happened in that church is applicable or transferable to other churches today. My challenge with talking about the growth of the Cathedral is that I was too busy during my time there trying to keep up with that growing community to analyze why or how it happened. I am clearly not an academic or a scholar, so it never occurred to me to do that analysis until I was asked to teach and consult and write about it. Can this be reproduced? Will the principles transfer to another time and place?

I honestly didn't know. So, in March of 2011, I accepted a call to be the senior pastor of Virginia-Highland Church in Atlanta, Georgia. Senior pastor was a lofty title for a position that didn't even pay a salary. In exchange for a free pastor, they agreed to become my lab to test out what I thought I knew about growing a church. They were saints, but they also were desperate. The average attendance during the months before I arrived was in the 20s. The church had no endowment, savings, or money with which to pay a pastor. That was fine with me because I already had a full-time job doing congregational renewal as a consultant and an adjunct seminary professor. I traveled almost every week, so what I was going to be able to do for them was bound to be limited. Because they had little to give and nothing to lose, we all laughed and decided to give it a try.

At first nothing happened. I have to say that I spent my first summer in a new city, a new home, and a new church just a bit depressed. What if I really didn't know anything about growing a church today? What if mainline churches really couldn't be revived? What if the Vintage Church couldn't be plugged in to the 21st century? Not only was I afraid I might let down Virginia-Highland Church, I also had no business traveling around the country teaching something that wasn't working in my own setting. Then, after about six months, something clicked. It was subtle at first, but new life suddenly began to break out. To be clear, the church hasn't grown as fast or as much as I had hoped, but by the three-year-mark attendance had quadrupled; we had completely restored a building that was in desperate condition; and they had begun talking about paying their pastor. Perhaps the key to reviving a mainline church is keeping your pastor on the road.

As I look at what has been the key to this turnaround, the primary answer can only be worship. I fly home late on Saturday night almost every week to preach and lead worship. That has been the one area in which I have been most engaged and where I have invested what little bit of time I have had. It also should be observed that this is an area where I have had to learn the most. It would be wonderful to report all I have learned about 21st-century worship, but, frankly, it would be miraculous just to get most congregations acquainted with worship appropriate for the last half of the 20th century.

Almost 200 volunteers made worship happen every week at the Cathedral of Hope. We had a great volunteer choir, a huge orchestra, well-trained ushers and greeters, acolytes, Eucharistic ministers, liturgists, accompanists, ensembles, hosts, a television studio, sound and light techs, and a myriad of other unpaid ministers who created, what one magazine reporter called, "worship with a capital W." At Virginia-Highland Church we had none of that, and I mean NONE. We had a few exhausted deacons, a piano that wouldn't stay tuned, and an electronic organ so old that the power cord caught fire one Sunday. We didn't have a single greeter or usher, but someone was drafted each Sunday.

I'd fly back to Atlanta from leading a workshop or conference or teaching a class and immediately scramble to get things ready for Sunday morning. On the way home from the airport, we often would stop by the grocery store to buy refreshments for the next day, as well as bread, wine, and grape juice for communion. My spouse was quickly pressed into service and, in the early days, served as the altar guild, usher, greeter, and hospitality committee. While I got the service parts ready, he was busy cleaning the sanctuary and fixing the coffee.

There were even Sundays when he was drafted to serve communion and play the organ. No wonder we were exhausted and depressed that first summer.

We had a small choir that was fairly typical, faithful, and, at times, extraordinary, but the music wasn't going to revive that church. The service was historically liturgical in a sometimes funky way. Fortunately, they long had celebrated communion every Sunday, so that was one change I did not have to fight to implement. I am completely convinced that weekly communion is something every church should ponder. I know that if you are Lutheran, Episcopalian, or Disciples of Christ I'm preaching to the choir, but I'd gently suggest that you also are evidence against my belief that simply reclaiming more fully this vintage sacrament will lead to church renewal by itself.

The challenge for the whole church is to make the sacraments and other rituals and traditions deeply moving sacred moments in the life of the community. Virginia-Highland Church was celebrating communion every week when I arrived, but they still were dying. My job was to take that moment in each week's service and make it **seem** holy, transformational, radically inclusive, and completely awe-some. Of course, the sacraments are holy, but I'm not sure that matters if no one notices. Shouldn't an encounter with the Holy stimulate your spirit and enliven your soul? If it doesn't we may be doing it wrong.

It is stunning to me that the church has managed to make even those moments that we consider most sacred mundane, ritualistic, and hollow. As a former United Methodist pastor, who served communion, as prescribed, on the first Sunday of every month whether we needed to or not, I know that attendance often fell on those Sundays. I also know why. We would tack it on to the end of an already pedestrian worship experience and thereby accomplish two things: we would fulfill our ritualistic obligation and assure the congregation that the Baptists would beat them to brunch one Sunday a month. Getting out earlier was about the only thing that distinguished Methodists from Baptists in the South, and, on the first Sunday of every month, we even took that away without invoking the Holy.

When I was at the Cathedral of Hope we also celebrated the Eucharist at every service, even the midweek contemporary one. In the 22 years I was there, I can honestly say that not a single Sunday passed that someone didn't come down the aisle in tears. I often would look up from serving and see people in the pews dabbing their eyes or weeping openly. We finally took to putting boxes of tissues in the pews like they do in some Pentecostal churches. At the end of one communion service, shortly after I arrived in Dallas, we were singing a praise chorus as the song of thanksgiving (Remember: *Eucharist* means "thanksgiving."), and the congregation spontaneously rose to their feet, reached across the aisle, grasped hands, and lifted them into the air. That wasn't in the bulletin anywhere. No liturgist instructed them to do that. We who were clearing the altar and preparing to pray didn't know how to respond. It was an expression of pure spontaneous gratitude and joy for being unconditionally welcomed to the table of grace. Now it is a practice that congregation continues to this day, with or without the pastor's permission.

To paraphrase Jesus, who was paraphrasing the Torah in rebuking Satan, "Humans cannot live by their *head* alone." If I could communicate only one thing to the mainline church it would be that. People do not and will not return to church on Sundays to learn more about God. They have Google, and Beliefnet.com will provide them more religious information than they can possibly assimilate. If information was what they needed, they could sit at Starbucks on Sunday morning surrounded by their peers and the comforting smells of pastry and coffee and read all about God on their smart phones. If the church is going to reclaim them, we have to offer them, at the very least, the possibility of an **experience** of God, a touch of the Holy, an encounter with the Divine, an opportunity for transformation, an invitation to find a purpose for their lives that will last past sunset.

When we look at all that competes for people's time on Sunday morning, it generally isn't informational. They skip church to kayak, hike, cross country ski, cheer their child's soccer team, go to art festivals, create some art themselves. They have exchanged sitting in a pew for the chance of a real experience of life. Singing threadbare hymns with mediocre accompaniment, listening to 20-minute lectures that seem to bore even the preacher, and numbly walking through the same ritual yet again cannot compete with living, and, frankly, I don't blame them for choosing to avoid most churches on Sundays.

Of course, I am not saying anything that hasn't been said to you and your church a thousand times before. What I am saying, though, is this: Virginia-Highland Church and dozens of other Vintage Churches have found a way to compete that gets people out of bed and into our sanctuaries, and, if we can do it, so can you. Here is how:

Give up classism.

Yes, we are smart, erudite, well read, sophisticated, coolly intellectual, and full-fledged members of America's intelligentsia. You don't need to prove you have advance degrees, even if they aren't fully paid for yet. Once upon a time the pastor was the best read and the most educated person in the village. That is no longer true, but the model of church built on that assumption seems to persist.

I don't mean to be unkind or rude, but I cannot for the life of me understand why our mostly white Euro-American denominations insist on making faith a largely intellectual exercise. Most of our African-American counterparts recognize the importance of embodied and experiential worship. Is our refusal to learn the value of this latent racism? Evangelical churches and immigrant churches know how to worship with their hearts, souls, bodies, and strength while we restrict our worship to only our minds. Is that because we are from a higher class than them? YES! I'm sorry, but mainline churches' left-brained approach to worship is, to a great extent, about class. It is time we confess it and repudiate it. It is so ironic that the churches that are most concerned about the poor and the economically and racially marginalized also are the most likely to worship as though we have nothing to learn from those for whom we claim to care so much.

As was said of critic Irving Howe, "Enthusiasm is not the enemy of intellect." No, we don't have to be artificially expressive, energetic, and passionate in worship, but do you remember the last time you cheered at a ballgame or rose to your feet to applaud a concert? When was the last time a song, or a story, or a book, or a movie brought you to tears? When did you last find yourself awed or get chill bumps at the sight of a sunset or a mountain vista? Do you remember the emotions that welled through you when you first held your child or grandchild? Why can't we bring some of that holiness and wholeness to church? Why can't worship offer some of that to people who are desperately seeking a tender touch from God?

We of the spiritual intelligentsia work tirelessly and diligently to craft sermons that say exactly what we want to communicate … to the congregant's brain. We write prayers and liturgy that is crafted to inspire the intellect of our community. We select each word so that it might lodge itself in the listener and be recalled at some point in the days ahead. Why can't we give at least as much energy, time, and devotion to crafting an **experience** they won't forget?

Take traditional (vintage) elements of worship and infuse them with new life, meaning, and energy.

Because the Cathedral of Hope was filled with people from every possible tradition who had left, or been rejected by, their churches, we approached every Sunday as though everyone in the room was there for the very first time. Each element in the service was clearly labeled and explained. Although we had screens for multimedia, we still used bulletins because it made visitors feel more comfortable to have a menu they could refer to and anticipate what was ahead in this new kind of church. We crafted the bulletin specifically for first-time visitors and avoided using terms that were unfamiliar or that we didn't explain. If we used liturgical or insider language, we always would explain what it meant so that everyone felt invited inside, enriched, and informed. This allowed them to hear and read words they might have known once without feeling ignorant or excluded. We discovered that sharing "insider language" and "code words" actually enhanced the feeling of welcome.

While it is different if the new folks are truly "unchurched," we discovered that most of those we attracted were what we called "post-church." Because of this, we worked very hard to help people reclaim the faith they might have lost along the way, but in new and life-giving ways. In Dallas, and now in Atlanta, many, if not most, of our members grew up in conservative Protestant or Catholic settings. If we read scriptures or sang songs that mention things like "sin" and "salvation," we made a conscious effort to reframe those ideas in liberating ways rather than avoiding or dismissing them.

Although we used lots of special themes and seasonal worship, I still worked hard at using the lectionary during those series. I remember one young woman whose family had refused to let her come home until she repented of being a lesbian. She dutifully called her parents every Sunday afternoon, and one week, during the course of the conversation, her mother mentioned what her Lutheran pastor had preached about that morning. As it turned out, because we, too, followed the Common Lectionary, I had preached from the same text. They got to comparing notes about the sermons and found the conversation relaxed and more open than it had been in months. Eventually, comparing sermon notes became a routine. The young woman confessed that she suspected that her mother was using it to check if she really went to church that week, but it left her feeling affirmed and more confident in her church's (and pastor's) legitimacy, even when I interpreted the scripture in dramatically different ways than her mother's pastor did.

Another way we adapted vintage liturgy for new and much younger congregants was to make as much of it as musical as possible. White Western worship is filled with too many words and too little singing. Rather than a long, wordy confession that no one would remember by the time they got to the parking lot, we sought more contemporary songs that were honest about our need for healing, help, forgiveness, and grace. We would sing them for a season, until members would say that, whenever they felt guilty or ashamed for something they had said or done during the week, that song would rise up and sing itself in their heart. They would remember they are forgiven and had an opportunity to change their ways and try again.

During one season at Virginia-Highland Church, we used a song from the Iona Community as the call to prayer. We generally change liturgical elements like this seasonally so they don't lose their power. We sing them long enough for the congregation to learn them, but not so long that they grow tired of them. Then, several months later, a young African-American college student stopped me during coffee hour to ask when we were going to sing that song again. I looked puzzled, not knowing which one he meant. He sang a bit for me in a beautiful tenor voice, and I realized he meant the song from Iona. When a piece of liturgy lodges itself like that in a young person you know your service is doing its work. He couldn't quote a word of the prayer I prayed that day or the sermon I preached, but something in him longed to return to a liturgical touchstone we had offered him.

In the introduction, I mentioned that, in my desk, I have a black phone handset, much like my grandmother used. (Hers was avocado.) It looks and feels just like hers, but the technology inside has been radically adapted so that it works with my smart phone, which has more computing power than the systems that took the first humans to the moon. That is the secret to invigorated vintage worship. It may have the same ancient or familiar form, but it functions in new, relevant, contemporary, and powerful ways. We can adapt our liturgy so that we preserve the value, history, and beauty, while letting it become a spiritual anchor for a new generation. If we do not, then, like my grandmother's old black rotary phone, our liturgies and traditions will be preserved in the museums of a few dying endowed churches to be read about by future generations. There was nothing wrong with my grandmother's phone. It was a gift through which I talked to her every week for almost half a century. It deserves neither criticism nor scorn. It deserves to be preserved and reinvented because the technology wasn't what was valuable; the connection was. If we can adapt our liturgy so that it becomes a connecting point for the next generation we will have served them well.

Ask different questions about the service of worship you are creating.

In seminary, we were trained to ask what we want the congregation to remember from the service/sermon. What that question means is what is it that we are going to say that we want remembered? That is the Western educational bias into which we all have been immersed.

What if, instead, we ask, on Wednesday, when members of the congregation are making plans for the weekend, and they think back to the previous Sunday, what do we want them to **feel**?

Do we want people to leave the sanctuary feeling more hope, and less guilt and shame, feeling more loved, and capable of loving more? Do we want people to leave feeling challenged, inspired, and determined to confront injustice? Do we want them to feel such an overwhelming compassion that they must do something to help the hurting? Do we want them to go out the doors so filled with awe that they cannot help but see the hand of God in every encounter with beauty and genuine humanity? Or do we want them to recall the meaning of some Greek word?

When I went to Dallas in 1987 I arrived the same day that Dr. Timothy Seelig arrived to become the artistic director of the Turtle Creek Chorale. We began our work in a community that was, in every way, overwhelmingly depressed. It was the worst of the AIDS crisis in Dallas, and he and I were both working with organizations made up of mostly gay men and, in my case, lesbian women. During the years that followed our arrival, despite the Turtle Creek Chorale and the Cathedral of Hope losing hundreds of key leaders, volunteers, donors, and friends to HIV/AIDS, both organizations flourished and grew. The Cathedral grew to become the largest church in the world, and in history, with a predominantly lesbian and gay membership, and the only progressive megachurch in the South. The Chorale grew to become the largest gay men's chorus in the country, and one of the premier choral groups of any kind.

At the peak of our organizations' lives, the Cathedral had to rent the Meyerson Symphony Center for our Christmas and Easter services. Although it seated more than 2,200, we still had to hold multiple services to accommodate the crowds on those holy days. We would have 3-4,000 in attendance. The Chorale also used the Symphony Center for their concerts. At Christmas they would fill the place five or six times.

As remarkable as it was that a liberal megachurch in Dallas, Texas attracted thousands for worship, I found it equally stunning that more than 8,000 people would pay to hear gay men sing Christmas songs. What Tim Seelig accomplished with the Turtle Creek Chorale was amazing. Tim and I arrived in Dallas on the same day, and we left Dallas at nearly the same time. He went on to become the artistic director of the San Francisco Gay Men's Chorus. At the end of our time in Dallas, as we transitioned from the Cathedral of Hope and the Turtle Creek Chorale, Tim and I worked together at an organization that I founded in 2004 called Hope for Peace & Justice. Tim led a program called Art for Peace & Justice.

I asked him one day about the secret to his phenomenal success with the Turtle Creek Chorale. I said, "So, just between us, with no false modesty, how did you do it? Are you really the best choral conductor?"

"Nope," he said, "I'm good at what I do, and I enjoy it, but there are other conductors who are more technically accomplished and skilled than I am."

"Then how did you do it? How did you create a phenomenon where thousands of Texans would come to hear mostly gay men sing?"

Without pausing, he gave me an answer he obviously had thought about before, for which few others even had been curious enough to ask. "At every concert, I gave every audience three experiences every time. They laughed, they cried, and they got chill bumps."

I can't help but wonder if that isn't a formula for filling our churches again. What kind of **experience** do you want people to have on Sunday mornings? What will be the high energy moments? At what points will the service feel pensive and reflective? What will move people to tears, to passion, to devotion, to celebration? When will the community share a laugh that expresses the joy they know in being together? What will move their hearts with compassion? Will there be a time of grieving or solidarity? How will the service facilitate genuine repentance rather than merely a rote prayer that passes through the brain and out the mouth, but never reaches the soul? When are they most likely to encounter the Holy, the Other, the Divine? How will their hearts and souls be changed and their spirits lifted? What will you do to make this the most memorable and meaningful experience of their week? How do you create a sense of awe and wonder in that space?

It seems to me that we need to consider these questions at least as seriously as we consider these others: What am I going to preach about? Who is ushering? What is the anthem? **What EXPERIENCE are you and the worship team seeking to craft for the people who will gather this Sunday?**

To answer that question adequately, we deliberately invited people to help plan worship who were not clergy or musicians. A former magician was the most creative addition to our team. He knew how to make the last light of a Tenebrae service extinguish itself, and how to make the baptismal fountain burst into flames on Pentecost Sunday. When it seemed the Gospel lesson was talking about "the bread of life" for the 12th Sunday in a row, someone else on the team borrowed a bread maker and put it in the sanctuary to run all Saturday night. The next morning everyone's mouths watered and stomachs growled, much like the impoverished congregation so long ago who heard Jesus say, "I am the Bread of Life." On the first Sunday of December, when the choir sang an anthem written by a member of our church who had died of AIDS, the lights suddenly dimmed and a 35-foot red AIDS ribbon was projected on the front of the sanctuary reminding everyone that, although it was Advent, it also was World AIDS Day.

Annie Dillard, in her book *Teaching a Stone to Talk*, said this about worship:

> *On the whole, I do not find Christians, outside of the catacombs, sufficiently sensible of conditions. Does anyone have the foggiest idea what sort of power we so blithely invoke? Or, as I suspect, does no one believe a word of it? The churches are children playing on the floor with their chemistry sets, mixing up a batch of TNT to kill a Sunday morning. It is madness to wear ladies' straw hats and velvet hats to church; we should all be wearing crash helmets. Ushers should issue life preservers and signal flares; they should lash us to our pews. For the sleeping god may wake someday and take offense, or the waking god may draw us out to where we can never return.*

If you will design 52 deliberately powerful, moving, inspiring, energetic, passionate, hope-filled worship services I promise you your church will thrive. That is why, as you anticipate EVERY service, you should ask:

- What do we want people to feel in this service?
- What visual images should they take away?
- What should they smell or taste?
- What do we want them to hear replaying throughout the week?
- What kind of experience are you trying to craft?
- Who do you want them to be as a result?
- What do we want people to go out and do as a result of having worshiped God?

If you seriously engage those questions then some of those who wander into your sanctuary for the first time just might come back the next Sunday wanting more, and, frankly, that is the ONLY way to revive a church, vintage or otherwise.

Remember, when it comes to worship, "One size fits SOME."

Most pale-skinned western Protestants were educated in a wordy world. We were taught to read as early as possible, and almost everything my generation learned we either read or heard spoken to us. Learning this way was rewarded and reinforced well into adulthood. Subsequent pedagogical approaches recognized that, although some of us, indeed, are auditory learners, others are visual. That is they need to see something to retain and integrate it. Still others of us are primarily tactile or kinesthetic learners, so we need to have some sort of emotional connection to the material. Of course, the truth is that all of us learn in all three of these ways and learn best when all three are present. Still, American higher education and religion seem to believe that people learn by being talked at.

This cultural arrogance of communication and learning styles continues to dominate the white, mainline Protestant church in America. Worship is an hour of words spoken, or read, or occasionally sung, generally to tunes so familiar that they have long been stripped bare of any cultural connection. The visual variation is generally restricted to paraments that rotate from red to green to white to purple. Some churches have gotten daring enough to use blue, but, even for them, an unfortunate shade of green generally serves for half the year. Advent, Christmas, and Easter see some variation, and fully half the congregation must assume that this is how the sanctuary looks all the time because Christmas and Easter are about the only times they show up.

Some renewing churches are doing a great job of beginning to incorporate visual art into worship. If we pastors can get our act together and plan things in advance, there are tremendous resources and entire teams of people willing to transform the church so that the worship experience is congruent and impactful. Art always has served the church well, but American Protestantism seemed determined to strip worship down to words as the only means to encounter the Word. It is important to remember that people will encounter God through what they see and feel as much as what they hear. What would a service be like if we gave what is seen and felt the same attention we give to what is going to be said and read?

Stained glass, paintings, and sculpture were the artistic ways the church sought to communicate to a population in which illiteracy was the norm. The church got creative and visual. That art is imbued with beauty, energy, and pathos and often designed for contemplation, devotion, and prayer. Modern church architecture might imitate some of those ancient aesthetics, but we rarely have sought to translate all of that to an age in which most people can read, but are as illiterate of the biblical story and the values of Jesus as those who cannot.

For most of its history, Virginia-Highland Church was a Southern Baptist congregation. As that denomination became increasingly conservative and even fundamentalist, Virginia-Highland Church became increasingly estranged. Eventually, the denomination bade them farewell because the church decided to ordain women as deacons. A few years later, the Georgia Baptist Convention of the Southern Baptist Church decided the church had to go because they were welcoming lesbian and gay people into their fellowship. Today it is a part of the United Church of Christ, where both of those things are pretty normative and certainly no impediment to membership.

The exterior of Virginia-Highland Church's building still looks like a typical southern Baptist church: red brick, white columns, and a central steeple. Large windows in the sanctuary are frosted but plain, and there are pews, a high barrel-vaulted ceiling, and columns. Except for the immersion baptistery in the front, which is never used, the interior looks for all the world like a plain New England meeting house. When I arrived, despite their season of decline, the sanctuary was in pristine condition except for one wall that had water damage. The exterior, however, looked as though the windows might fall out at any time, or as if the steeple might fall off … and part of it did. The air conditioning, which is as critical in the South as heat is in the North, literally was held together with swimming pool tape. It died at the end of my first summer there. The sanctuary seats approximately 300, but the church does not have a single off-street parking space. It was built during a time when people walked to church, and the residential neighborhood made the church vital and alive. Filling that space with worshippers again seemed like a worthy but daunting challenge, especially for a very part-time pastor.

Today the building is not full, except on Easter, but the weekly congregation is larger than it has been in many decades. There are several factors that account for that, but I believe the primary one is the worship experience we create for people every Sunday morning. Our philosophy is *something for everyone, but everything for no one.* What I mean is that no single demographic or segment of the congregation determines how we worship. New members know that there are parts of every service they aren't really going to like, but there are other parts that will move their souls. They also know that those parts will be different for their neighbors in the pew. There has been a shift in the core value of the congregation so members now see themselves as the hosts of worship, not the consumers. That may be our greatest accomplishment of all.

We work every week to include as many different styles of music as will fit congruently in 70 minutes. We will do a classic European hymn, but it may be preceded by a Black gospel introit and followed by a call to prayer from Taizé or Vietnam. We likely will sing a piece of contemporary Christian music as the gradual and a raucous African Gloria or doxology. Using nontraditional music in a liturgical context creates diversity and invites the congregation to be open to new experiences. With each liturgical season we change out all the parts of the service, though most of the form remains consistent enough that people know what to expect when they invite family or friends to join them. Remember: "One size fits SOME."

While my Episcopal readers are having apoplexy about the idea of changing the liturgy seasonally, we have discovered several great values in varying worship components and using a wide variety of music styles:

- It allows for greater diversity in worship, which tends to attract a more diverse congregation. We in the dominant culture need to open our hearts to hear life's song sung to a different beat. Perhaps that will free us from simply talking about diversity to actually building a diverse community.
- In leading liturgy, with preaching and presence, energy is the key. If music doesn't move people to devotion, excitement, contemplation, or tears then perhaps it is best left out.
- It appeals to a younger congregation that might be seeking vintage worship but also has a great value for other cultures and for variety. Worship feels stable but not boring or repetitive.
- It helps reinforce the congregation's hospitality. Every time we sing a Southern gospel hymn my most progressive member thanks me for reminding him that he is a host and not a guest and that he is part of a community in which he comes to serve, not just be served, because he hates that kind of music.
- Finally, although I discovered it quite accidentally, I found that a congregation in which worship changes on a regular basis is much more open to other changes. In most settings if you can change worship and survive then you can change just about anything.

Stained-Glass Windows

The final and perhaps most valuable thing we did at Virginia-Highland Church was to install new "stained-glass windows." Not literal windows, but, shortly after I arrived at VHC, we installed two very large flat-screen televisions on either side of the chancel. It is my conviction that using media in worship is equivalent to the use of art and stained glass to tell the story to a preliterate society.

I'll admit the new TVs were horrendously unattractive in that pristine and classic sanctuary. The members could rightly accuse me of marring the aesthetic of their church. Frankly, the unattractive nature of this addition was deliberate. I announced from the outset that this was an experiment, so we bought two large but inexpensive TVs. We put them on the floor on tables that came from IKEA. This church had no money so, fortunately, I was able to get TVs donated. We covered the tables with plain black tablecloths that we hoped made them disappear as much as possible.

The images on the screen were created on a laptop using PowerPoint. The laptop, which, at the time, had to sit on the organ in the choir loft on the chancel, was operated by someone sitting on the front pew with a remote control. It was very rudimentary but apparently effective. Again, I reminded people that this was an experiment and that it really hadn't cost the church anything. The older, original members didn't love them, but they tolerated them. I was still on my honeymoon, and they didn't pay for the TVs or for me.

The other reason they tolerated them, and eventually raised the money to install a much more attractive and effective system, was the impact was almost immediate. Younger people visited, and now they returned. I had arrived in March and endured the summer with few signs of growth or new life. The screens were installed in the late fall. At Christmas I tried an experiment with a 5 p.m. children's service. Since the congregation had only two kids, I didn't want to ask the music director to invest a lot of energy in a service that I anticipated would have five or six people in attendance. I prepared the entire service on PowerPoint, including the children's carols, and ran it all myself. As it turned out, 37 people attended, all but two of them guests. The kids loved the music and Christmas story told on the screens, and the parents were relieved that they didn't have to try to keep their kids quiet for a traditional service that simply had been adapted for children.

One of the families that visited that night told me that they had just moved to the city and were church shopping. They made it clear that, ultimately, the kids were the ones who would decide where they attended. We didn't see them again for months, but then they came again one Sunday morning. I explained that we had a children's program that took place during the worship hour, but they said the kids were the ones who wanted to come back to a regular service. As it turned out, the use of media in the service was what persuaded this family to choose our church over all the others they visited. They explained that it wasn't artificially intergenerational worship, which they thought too often feels contrived and leaves everyone unhappy; it was a place in which the kids could learn the Christian tradition without being bored or thinking it was only ancient history.

The critical point is that this family was a tipping point for the congregation. In fact, as I write this, one of those parents is the president of the congregation, and the other is the chair of our communication team. One of the kids read the Gospel for Easter Sunday service. Fortunately, other families have followed, including a large African-American family who stated flatly that the reason they joined was that we used diverse images on the screens and, though the face their kids saw preaching was white, they constantly were seeing biblical images and art with people of color. One of the parents in that family now serves as our treasurer.

I know mainline churches resist the idea of introducing multimedia into worship for lots of good reasons, but let me give the reasons I believe it is critical:

- An older man gave the money for screens in his 150-year-old sanctuary in Minnesota and said, "I want my grandkids to come back to church, and every time I see them their face is buried in a screen of some sort. When I was a kid my face was always buried in a book. The world has changed, and the church needs to change with it." If we are serious about attracting millennials, we have to prove that we are willing to communicate to them in the way they need to hear/see/learn/feel the Gospel. In the United Church of Christ, we like to say, "No matter who you are or where you are on life's journey, you are welcome here." If we are honest we would add, "So long as you want to worship the way your grandparents did."
- As I mentioned above, technology and diverse music are tools we can use to be an authentically diverse congregation. When I arrived at Virginia-Highland it was essentially an all-white congregation. They were a mixture of gay and straight, but they were almost all white. My

white family joining didn't enhance the diversity. Our church is only a couple of miles from Dr. Martin Luther King, Jr.'s grave in the city that was home to the civil rights movement, so it seemed sinful to me that we were still a one-race church. I wanted to avoid the kind of contrived diversity that would have come from asking our white choir to sing black spirituals accompanied by a 50-year-old organ. The only tools I had at the beginning were the stories I told and the images I showed.

We use the art of "Jesus Mafa" to illustrate the Gospel almost every Sunday. The children of our church are growing up with African images of Christ, and that is a transformational paradigm shift. Our church is not nearly as racially diverse as I hope it will become, but a remarkable number of our new members have been Asian, Hispanic and African-American. The music and the media are 100 percent responsible for that. Almost all mainline churches SAY the right thing, but that is not enough to make diversity more than a value for which we dream.

- Jesus used ordinary objects and visuals of what was around him to illustrate the Gospel: seeds and showers, sheep and shepherds, etc. Think for just a moment about the percentage of time you spend looking at a screen every day. It is clearly one of the tools Jesus would use. He also told stories right out of the common culture. To do that with a new generation requires technology. I didn't want my daughters to grow up with only their father preaching about Dr. King. I wanted them to *hear* this prophet of God speak to them.

When Maya Angelou spoke for us at the Cathedral of Hope, I was proud to introduce her to my daughters. Long before that day, however, they had heard her offer the modern lesson during worship simply by playing a recording from a CD of her reading a passage from one of her books.

I can quote by heart the closing words of that beautiful movie *A River Runs Through It*, but it is much more powerful for the congregation to watch the water flow and hear its song when the narrator says:

> *Eventually, all things merge into one, and a river runs through it. The river was cut by the world's great flood and runs over rocks from the basement of time. On some of the rocks are timeless raindrops. Under the rocks are the words, and some of the words are theirs. I am haunted by waters.*

I encourage you to find that clip on YouTube and watch it while you remember your baptism and how your life has been haunted by waters.

I realize that some of you reading this will think I am suggesting that we install screens and sing with a bouncing ball like the evangelical megachurches we disdain. Well, I could make worse recommendations than learning from places that are attracting thousands of young people today, but that is not what I am prescribing. We do put the words of hymns and songs on the screens. It is easier for older people to read, and people sing better when their faces are not buried in hymnals.

However, we also print the hymns with music in the bulletins for those who read music and prefer a more traditional presentation. The screens in our sanctuary are sometimes used to play video clips because, in addition to using the lessons assigned by the lectionary, we often will have a modern lesson presented by someone like Dr. Angelou. Mostly, though, the screens present visual images of what is being said. They are an unobtrusive way to create a postmodern communication, which gives the viewer another way to interpret and, perhaps, internalize the Word or words that are being spoken. A story told about an old woman's courage takes on a very different meaning if the old woman on the screen is wearing a burka or the face of a Native American.

- I will acknowledge that preaching visually—finding images, thinking of what will be seen as well as heard—was not what I learned in seminary. By the time I arrived a Virginia-Highland Church, I had been preaching for nearly 40 years. What we are doing here is completely different than anything I have ever done. It challenges me and enriches me. I believe my preaching is the best it has ever been even though the congregation to which I preach is about the size of the choir in the last church I served. It has been a great gift to me, and visually illustrating my sermons has helped me to hear and see the Gospel in new and fresh ways. I knew nothing about technology, or even PowerPoint, before this, but if I can learn to do this anyone can.

- I do not mean this to be unkind to the wonderful people who provided music so faithfully at the church when I arrived, but, to say it plainly, we were very limited in what we could do well and with integrity. Creating music videos or using some of the myriad ones that exist on YouTube seemed totally natural and normal to the younger people whom we started attracting. In fact, it would have felt artificial to them had I tried to use a contemporary song sung by our robed choir accompanied by our organ or piano. When *their* music or favorite artist appears at their church on screens, they feel that this really is their church, too. Rather than tell the story of Moses in a basket in the Nile, I have paused while a clip from *Prince of Egypt* tells the story much better than I.

- Again, one size fits *some*. People learn differently. Miss Blanche has been a member of my church for almost all of its life and almost all of hers. She joined in the 1920s. Although she was a bit testy about me "marring the sanctuary" with screens, she thanked me for fixing the sound system. She talked animatedly about how much better she was able to hear the sermon. I didn't have the heart to tell her that it isn't the sound that has improved; rather, she is able to catch much more of the meaning when I put quotes on the screen or images to illustrate what I'm saying. Even though Blanche doesn't love the different styles of music or the use of videos for modern lessons, she loves that church. No one is more enthusiastic about its renewal, and no one is more supportive. Although she is well past 90, Blanche has been at worship more than any other member because she knows she is a host. If these changes attract new people to the Virginia-Highland family, she is all for it, whether she personally likes the changes or not.

Our multimedia production has been upgraded, but the church still doesn't have much money. We wanted to install flat screens properly and permanently, but it required relocating heating vents. (That was an extra $10,000.) In the end, we went to Costco and bought two 82" flat screens and mounted them on the kind of poles you see in airports and convention centers. We thought we would use liturgical banners to hide the poles but discovered that only called attention to them. The vertical lines of the pole disappear, and the screens seem to float. We moved the old, ugly TVs into the balcony so the choir and those on the chancel can see the images. We bought a new powerful laptop to run the screens and hired a technician to install it all. The total cost for it all was less than $10,000, and the result on Sunday morning is better in many ways than the multimedia experience at the Cathedral of Hope with its television studio and hundreds of thousands of dollars of equipment.

I know that is a lot of money for many churches, but we didn't spend it all at once. We got some of the equipment donated, and we adapted what we could. Still, how do you measure the value of these changes in terms of the families with preteen kids who have started to attend? We have tried to start a program for that age group that runs concurrent with Sunday worship, but they refuse to leave the sanctuary. How many churches have that problem with youth?

Although I am a true believer in multimedia in worship, there is no set formula for effective preaching or worship. Whatever style or pattern you may use, pay attention to energy, enthusiasm, passion, and pathos. Whatever the style, if your worship doesn't move, challenge, stir, motivate, inspire, cheer, or in some way transform people then it won't attract them, and they'd probably do better finding some other way to spend their Sunday morning. An encounter with God should never leave us unchanged. If your worship service isn't an opportunity for transformation then they should find someplace that is.

Chapter Four
Structured for a Wiki World

In the 1970s I attended the South Georgia Annual Conference of the United Methodist Church. I was in high school at the time and had been elected as a youth delegate. It was a nice idea, in theory, but I spent the entire week being bored, confused, or lost.

The most confusing moment came at the very end of the conference. The last act of business in those days was for the bishop to read the appointments of clergy to their new churches. Appointed for only one year, every United Methodist clergy had to be reappointed at every annual conference. The bishop would read the name of the clergyperson (mostly men in those days) and then the name of the church to which they were being sent for the next year. As with every other mainline denomination, this was a transitional time for the Methodists who, until that time, generally assigned a pastor to a church four consecutive times before moving them on. This itinerant system was still in place in South Georgia, and, in just a couple of years when I was 18, the bishop would read my name, appointing me as a student pastor to a circuit of three small rural churches.

The appointing of a pastor, though a solemn and sacred process, was interesting only to the pastor and the church, and, then, mostly in the hope that the bishop would not mispronounce your name or, in the case of Bishop William Cannon, that he would not make some extemporaneous remark about you or the church. That Friday, though, the boredom was broken when the bishop sonorously read a name and then a church and the room was startled by a woman's soft scream. I looked at the older folks seated on either side of me for an explanation, and one older pastor patted me on the knee and said simply, "I guess she didn't know that they were moving."

Horrified, I whispered, "Can they do that?"

"Oh yes," he said, nodding his head, "that was how it used to be for us all every year. You never knew until your name was read if you would be moving by next Thursday or staying."

Of course, it is inconceivable, even in a hierarchical system, that a pastor or congregation would be treated that way today. Every Protestant church is much more mutual, collegial, and congregational in structure, function, and expectations. This is a good thing on almost every level.

The irony, though, is that the culture is making this more egalitarian way of being church a challenge. The rapid pace of change, the torrent of information flowing at us, and the frantic fullness of people's lives all make a genuinely and fully consultational process for decision making ineffectual, if not plainly impossible.

In ages past, it was possible for people to have a series of meetings to ensure that everyone was consulted and everyone's voice was heard. This is a core value for many of us in congregational churches. Today, however, the reality is that few important decisions allow the luxury of that much time. By the time the church has a series of meetings most contemporary decisions are irrelevant.

Further, to speak bluntly, the only people who really have time to participate in those meetings are people who are retired empty-nesters. Young families working two jobs and raising children simply do not have the time to attend meetings, or must do so at a cost to their families. The result is that a small group of people "wear too many hats" and participate in what is increasingly pseudo-congregationalism. The danger with this artificial form of congregationalism today is that it causes us to miss the point and value of a genuinely egalitarian process.

Younger families feel unheard and marginalized because their only option is to attend another meeting, find another babysitter, and miss another recital or soccer game. After a time they lose interest in the church or simply diminish the level of their investment in decision-making. The church is deprived of their perspective, values, and passion, and management becomes the domain of only a few. We pretend this is congregationalism.

So, how does a Vintage Church retain its values around decision-making while thriving in, what I like to call, a white-water world, a world that is moving at a perilous rate of speed? Perhaps we might gain some insight by comparing how the old multi-volume encyclopedias have been replaced by Google and Wikipedia.

When many of us were kids, our parents made a significant investment in a large set of multi-volume books that sat ponderously on shelves in our home. When we needed to know something or write a report, we would pull down the appropriate volume and read until we found the information that we needed. Unfortunately, by the time my youngest brother came along nine years later, much of the information was out of date. My mother asked recently what she was supposed to do with "my" encyclopedias. She went on to remind me how when I was a kid I would spend the summer reading them from cover to cover. (Once a nerd …) Still, even I don't want them. Who has the time when you can type a word or two into a search engine and have more information than you can ever read?

Wikipedia is visited daily by millions of people seeking to read one of their five million articles, which are written and edited by the public. Time and again, Wikipedia has been proven more accurate, current, and relevant than materials that have traditionally been published by "experts." (Perhaps we need a church renewal Wikipedia, but, then, who would buy my books?)

The word "wiki" still doesn't appear in many dictionaries because it is such a new concept. It generally refers to open-source software or web applications that allow, according to Wikipedia, "collaborative modification, extension, or deletion of its content and structure." What would a Wiki-Church look like?

We congregationalists resist top-down governance with all our might. That often gets actualized by disempowering the pastor and staff in favor of concentrating management and decision-making in the hands of the small number of people who show up for meetings. The first step to changing this is acknowledging that the congregational system isn't. It has become a system of governance by a relatively small group of people who circulate the positions among themselves and complain that new members and young people won't take responsibility.

While this statement will offend some and anger others, it is a truth that needs to be spoken if the way we manage and govern our Vintage Churches is going to be brought into the 21st century. We must stop having meetings, at least in the ways we always have. The truth is that much of how the church functions is to meet the emotional and relational needs of retired empty-nesters. Make no mistake, these are the saints who fund the church and do most of the work and ministry. I do not intend to denigrate them in any way; in fact, my intent is to acknowledge that the church exists because of them and owes them a debt, repayable by meeting their needs and honoring their contribution. Having said that, though, it is important that we not try to honor them or help them find meaning and community through how we govern our churches.

Being together in meaningful ways is a critical need of every human. When your children have moved out, and you have retired from a significant job, that need often gets filled by the church. That is how it should be. That, however, is not congregationalism. If the church is going to be an agile, adaptive, improvisational institution, we must find other ways to make decisions that invite younger voices to be heard and allows them to engage with tools they are accustomed to using, which are mostly virtual.

During my first four years at Virginia-Highland Church the congregation more than quadrupled in size, but the number of meetings we held was reduced by three-fourths. The parish council does at least 75 percent of their work via email and gathers less frequently for much shorter meetings. The important work gets done in meetings open to everyone following the worship service. They don't have to sit through reports that could have been read at home, but they can be invited to engage in the vision and mission of the church. Early on, the council adopted an agenda with three items: finances, facilities, and future. The agreement was to spend 50 percent of our time talking about the future and never to meet for more than 90 minutes.

When I arrived at the church, the bylaws had more pages than the church had members. Through a grassroots process, we reduced those 27 pages to six. That rather radical proposal was then distributed electronically and by print to the entire congregation. Significant feedback was offered, and changes were made. Almost 100 percent of the feedback came virtually, and almost no one attended the forum that was held after worship one Sunday. When the feedback was incorporated finally, and the finished product distributed, the bylaws were approved unanimously one Sunday in less than a minute between the closing hymn and the benediction. The entire congregation had been consulted and heard.

The church then developed new vision and mission statements through small-group studies, which generated the content that was shaped by a vision team. This team met in person only a couple of times and did most of their work virtually with email, Skype, and GoToMeeting-type technology. They reported their conclusions to the parish council via email, and the report then was distributed to the entire congregation the same way. The vision and mission statements were published in the bulletin for a couple of weeks, and feedback solicited. Two words were tweaked, and not a single person attended the open forum the vision team offered. Without dissent, in less than one minute, the church adopted revolutionary new vision and mission statements at the end of Sunday worship.

Everyone felt heard, not just those who had babysitters or the time to attend a series of meetings. By repeated opportunities to provide feedback in a variety of ways, the decision was genuinely congregational and had incredible feedback. Every member of Virginia-Highland Church can tell you what its mission is because they genuinely own it. They see it as their instructions to the leadership—both pastoral and elected—about what we are to do and how we are to do it. Proof of this arrived when strong feedback was given to us about a proposed budget, which didn't seem to adequately reflect the new mission. While I disagree with the prioritization decisions that were made (underfunding music) I couldn't have been prouder that the congregation understood what a mission really means.

In a system in which vision and mission are owned and actualized, many decisions already have been made. We don't have to ask the congregation, or have a series of meetings, to determine their will. Because our vision and mission have been established by the congregation, they already have given us our marching orders, and the work of leadership is implementation.

Every year we have a congregational meeting/Christmas Party after church one Sunday. Forums are offered beforehand, and information is widely distributed virtually. The business part of the party is very brief, but the meeting is well attended. People leave feeling empowered because they were present. They adopt priorities and a budget for the coming year. Those decisions guide, inform, and direct every other decision that must be made. Fewer meetings are needed, and decisions are reached more quickly. We are able to report back to the congregation during the year about how their will is being implemented, and they know what we mean because they were ALL a part of expressing that will.

As I read the Gospels, I'm always impressed at Jesus' ability to adapt to a wide variety of situations and settings. In many ways, he was the epitome of an agile leader. He didn't simply repeat what he said or believe in the same way; he kept finding new ways to communicate and connect that were appropriate to the particular situation. In my opinion, agile leadership is possible only when clarity of vision, mission, and values is present. The leaders of a local church are free to make decisions and respond in innovative ways when they are clear about the direction, purpose, and guiding values. That is the real power of congregationalism. When a community expresses those things and participates in wiki-ways, the leadership doesn't need a long bureaucratic process to confirm what they already have been told is the will of the people. (Unless, of course, you are simply fearful and covering your behind.)

When Jesus moved from supporting a wounded person to confront a self-righteous religious leader, he did not have to step aside and consult with God. Jesus had done his work to determine God's will. At his baptism, Jesus heard the word "Beloved." He then spent a very intense 40 days and nights determining what that meant and how it ought to find expression. Once he was clear, the rest of his time was spent living out God's vision, mission, and values for his life. Oh, make no mistake; he spent time checking in and doing course corrections. He went aside for prayer and then returned to the valley to continue the ministry. Just imagine if Jesus had spent as much time, energy, and resources in management meetings as he did actually doing the ministry. How has the church, the body of Christ, missed this?

Please ignore what I am about to say if this is not true about your church, but it has been a problem in almost every congregational church with which I have consulted. They cannot make creative decisions or take risks in a timely manner. When Jennifer moved to town to take a new executive position she began attending a church in her new neighborhood. She loved the worship and the people. Mostly, though, she loved the vision and mission statement that the church recited as their creed every Sunday. She always had believed a church should be outwardly focused, and, frankly, the reason she attended was not so much her faith in God as it was her gratitude. She was so grateful for the blessed life that she had been given that she was determined to give some of her time and money back to people in need. This church seemed to share those values.

One day on her way to work, she passed a homeless woman and paused to give her a dollar. The woman thanked her but said that what she really needed was a shower. Puzzled, Jennifer stopped to talk to her. She learned that, as a result of living on the street and occasionally in shelters, the woman knew that she smelled. She was able-bodied, was willing to work, and had some skills she could use, but no one was going to hire someone who smelled bad. The conversation haunted Jennifer all day because she remembered that in the city in which she lived formerly a church opened the gym of a local school on Saturdays so that the homeless could bathe. They even tried to provide clean clothes for them. It was a transformational program.

Without hesitation, she knew that this was exactly the kind of ministry that reflected the core values her new church espoused. So, she picked up the phone and called her boss and asked for help. The company president had donated a good bit of money to the president of the local school board and give Jennifer his private number. Within an hour, she had succeeded in getting permission to run a trial program out of the school across the street from her new church. They agreed to do it for the summer when the kids were gone, and continue it for one year if it worked and then evaluate expanding to other schools around the city. The school board chair had been looking for some way to impact homelessness in the inner city around their schools.

The next Sunday, with a written proposal in her hand, Jennifer excitedly went to church. As they recited their mission statement during worship, the folder almost vibrated with witness that this was exactly what the church believed they were called to do. After the service, she knew she should wait, but she couldn't help but blurt out her idea to the pastor during coffee hour. The pastor also seemed thrilled with the possibilities and immediately introduced Jennifer to the council member who chaired the outreach committee. The committee chair took Jennifer's folder and promised to present it at the committee's next meeting. Unfortunately, that wasn't going to take place for a few weeks because they only met every other month. Then she explained that their recommendation would need to go to the deacons and finally to the council.

The next Sunday, the pastor looked for Jennifer during coffee hour, but she was not there. After she had missed three Sundays, the database triggered a phone call to Jennifer. The next Sunday, the deacon who made the call reported to the pastor and the chair of the outreach committee that they didn't need to do anything with Jennifer's proposal because she had given $100,000 to the local YWCA and they implemented the program immediately. She explained that, by the time the church decided, the summer would have passed. It was clear by their actions that they really didn't mean what they said, because they had put a system in place to ensure their mission never really got fulfilled unless it could be done in the way they always had done it.

This is a parable of why so many Vintage Churches are dying. No one can make a creative decision. Everyone, especially the pastor, is afraid to act without going through multiple layers of consultation and approval. This is largely done by volunteers and committees of retired empty-nesters when they have time to get together. In a white-water world, the pace of decision-making in the church is unacceptable.

If we want to be an agile church, we must adapt an attitude that empowers people to make decisions based on the vision and mission that the church has approved already. These new programs should almost always be short-term experiments to determine if something is worthwhile. These programming and ministry experiments should be low-cost and low-risk, with built-in opportunities to evaluate quickly and let them go if they are not effective. The image of whitewater decision making ought to be:

Ready.
Fire.
Aim.

Prepare, but do not over prepare. In a world in which situations are changing so rapidly, more will be learned by some controlled, low-risk, experimental firing than by a long season of study and preparation. Don't act prematurely, but the system should give permission to act quickly if:

- The ministry program is congruent with the vision and mission of the church.
- It expresses the core values of the congregation.
- It is low cost/risk.
- It can be evaluated as an experiment and either expanded or discontinued without recrimination.

Many congregations would benefit from taking the story of Jennifer and her great idea and walking through what would have happened had it been your church. Create a decision tree, and you may be shocked how ill prepared your congregation is to make decisions at the speed of the 21st century.

Chapter Five
Removing the "Lead" from Leadership

When my father wanted us boys to hurry up, he would tell us to "get the lead out." That common English idiom reflects, of course, the fact that he thought we were moving or acting as if we were weighted down. It is a phrase that can be aptly applied to many church leaders today. The sluggishness with which we respond implies that we have missed the enlivening, empowering, and energizing nature of the Spirit. Why? I've pondered this and have several theories.

A major weight or freezing factor in the church is fear. You would think that we are doing brain surgery and that one wrong move will kill or paralyze the patient. The truth is the church was here before us and will remain after us. Part of the strength of the Vintage Church, I believe, is a clear awareness that we did not invent this. We inherited it and wish to pass it on, but we are not making this up as we go along. We are a part of a durable institution that, despite its ups and downs, its highs and lows, is strong enough to survive even us. Why are we so afraid of making mistakes?

One shift that must be made in almost every church I know is to create a culture that allows for, encourages, and even celebrates mistakes. In a world in which we are encountering and embracing change at such a rapid rate, experimentation is the key to finding our way forward. By definition, an experiment is something with a high probability of failure but the kind of failure from which we will learn. In his book *The Agile Church*, Dwight Zscheile talks about taking tennis lessons. Balls launched into the net and over the fence were greeted by the instructor with the statement, "This is great. You are making good mistakes now." So, too, the church must be willing, even anxious, to make some good mistakes. Our tentativeness and hyper-caution will not serve us well in the face of rapid change.

Virginia-Highland Church was at the point of death. Had it not been for a preschool that paid 50 percent of the budget, they would have been forced to close their doors long before I arrived. Ironically, as I write this, the preschool has told us they are moving out. That loss of revenue will present a challenge, but not a life-threatening one. Part of the reason for the revitalization is that the congregation has embraced the experiments we have tried with grace and humor. Some have worked spectacularly; others not so much. No one has died, and no one has been executed when something failed.

Churches should write into their pastor's contract the requirement to have 12 failures a year. Unless there is an expressed expectation that leaders will try things that do not work, there will be an unexpressed fear that failures will be punished. We recently installed a new associate pastor. In the charge to her, the president of the congregation said:

> *Love the people you serve and the God who called you with every fiber of your being and you will find that you are loved in return more than you could ever have imagined. Pour out your energy with great passion*

*and you will soon discover the empowering Spirit of
God present in your life. Do not be distracted by little
things, for God has called you and empowers you to do
great things. Do not neglect your own relationship
with God for that will sustain you in the difficult and
trying days that come to us all.*

*Finally do not fail to make mistakes. If you do
not make mistakes then your work is too restrained and
it will never be greatly used by God. Dare to dream
great dreams and to believe the unbelievable is possible
with God. Ask forgiveness if you need to for mistakes
you have made, but never need to apologize for failing
to try. Remember it is God who thought so highly of
you as to trust you with this sacred ministry, never
allow anything to cause you to forget this moment
when you were consecrated to be a part of one of the
greatest works God is doing in our lifetime.*

After she made her vows to the congregation we offered the
following charge to the church:

*Beloved, you have chosen a servant, let her serve. You
have chosen a leader, let her lead you. You have chosen
a disciple of Christ, help her to remain so. Allow her as
one of your pastors to have new ideas and to try them
in your midst. Do not be anxious to quench those ideas.
Let the differences that arise be marked by understanding, respect, and with as much humor as possible. Let
our diversity be a bridge to lead us to our common purpose. Lend to her your encouragement. Don't assume
that someone else has already said "thanks" or "well*

done." As she ministers to others, you should minister to her. Have confidence in her as one called by God and through your faith in her have confidence also in the teachers who have taught her; the great minds whose work she has read and studied; the family of God who has nurtured her thus far; and in God who has chosen her and is not finished with her yet. The work is great, but our God is greater. With your love and God's power she cannot fail, and, if she stumbles, let us be the first to lift her up to try again.

Perhaps if all our pastors promised to make mistakes, and all our churches took a vow to lift them when they fail, we might find a way to be less tentative and fearful when trying to find new ways to do the work of grace on earth.

The other lead that weighs down too many leaders of Vintage Churches is that we may think the church needs to change, but seldom imagine that *we* do. Most seminaries are still teaching the same curriculum in the same way they did 50 years ago. They are equipping people to pastor churches of the 1960s and '70s. To paraphrase my mentor, the late Lyle Schaller, "If we wake up tomorrow and the world has managed to roll back the clock 40 years we are ready! But if we wake up tomorrow and it is well into the 21st century then we need to be about the work of retooling and reinvention."

A great danger in affirming the value of Vintage Church is that it leaves us with the illusion that what we always have done is sufficient, or that all we need to do is maintain old patterns long enough and they will come back in style. No, that vintage looking black handset that looks like my grandmother's phone has to function completely differently when I plug it into my iPhone. I watch how my daughters build outfits from the vintage clothes they love and realize that their grandparents would never recognize what they are wearing.

It is a challenge to always be learning new skills. The onslaught of new technology leaves me frustrated to the point of giving up. Every time I turn around there is a new program to learn or an app to download. The challenge is to know what is worth the investment of my time, what others can or should do, and what should be ignored completely. Still, what I do know is that reading information about technology, marketing, communication, demographic, and business trends is much more beneficial to the future of my congregation than reading theology. This isn't an either/or proposition; I simply am advocating for church leaders to boldly explore new fields and learn new skills. The Vintage Church needs to "plug into" the smartphone and all the other tools that people are using and by which they are being shaped.

One great holdback here is, again, our fear. We are embarrassed by what we don't know, and sometimes what we don't know is a lot. This should help us relate to our congregations. My mother stalks me on Facebook. Every time I call she knows where I am in the world because I have checked in. It is how my daughters keep track of me as well. I check in for that very purpose. It lets us all feel connected. While that may seem weird on several levels, here are three generations touching one another virtually. If my mother can learn a new skill for being a mother and grandmother, I suspect we all can.

In fact, one great ministry I have seen in a number of churches I work with has been focused around that very thing. Old Vintage Churches with underused rooms set up old, out-of-date computers that have been given to them. They invite older members of their congregations to come early or stay late so the youth can meet them to set up, update, or check their social media accounts. The youth, who often are far removed from their actual grandparents, are getting an experience that some would say is vintage, but they are getting it in an entirely new way. One young man told me that he felt guilty because he was helping this older man connect with his granddaughters, but all he did was complain about their piercings and tattoos. He was afraid he might be getting the grandchildren in trouble. What he actually was doing was witnessing how one generation perceives another and learning skills that might help him with his own parents or grandparents.

Technology has presented us with many challenges that the church must find new ways to address. It also has offered us a myriad of opportunities for doing ministry in new and authentic ways. None of this will happen, however, without church leaders being open to learn new skills and take new adventures. So let's get the lead out and lead with passion and possibilities.

Chapter Six
Finding our Voice

As a young child, I fell in love with the church that, in the 1960s, spoke up for civil rights and racial justice. Of course, not every church did; many defended the status quo and continued to be segregated themselves. Others, probably the majority, simply remained politely silent as though nothing was happening in the world. The churches that stirred my heart, though, gave voice to where I believe Jesus would have been found in that struggle, and allowed me to fall in love with an institution and a Savior. That church then largely disappeared, or its voice grew quiet or was drowned out by louder, more conservative voices that largely defined what it meant to be a Christian for more than a generation.

Even today, the conservative church and its political expression is why so many millennials define themselves as "spiritual but not religious." Survey after survey has revealed that less than 20 percent of people aged 16-29 have a favorable impression of the church. They believe the church is antigay, too judgmental, too involved with conservative politics, insensitive to those who are different, and not accepting of people of other faiths. (Barna Group, "A New Generation Expresses Its Skepticism and Frustration with Christianity") The truth is that most progressive Vintage Churches are not those things, but how would those young people know? It seems we have laryngitis, or somehow believe that articulating our differences to ourselves will be sufficient. It is not.

Many years ago I attended a small luncheon in Washington, D.C. at which Senator Edward Kennedy was an impromptu speaker. Actually, I think he simply was introduced at the luncheon and asked to say a few words, but, as far as I was concerned, he delivered the ultimate message that day. Speaking without notes and with a weakened voice, he articulated most powerfully an image that still guides my thoughts about the mainline church. He spoke of politics, of course, but what I heard speaks loudly to churches and to the reality so many of us are facing today.

The Republicans had just taken control of the government. Although the nation seemed almost evenly divided, the Republicans had won. Acknowledging that there were many reasons for that, Senator Kennedy singled out one challenge that he said threatened to make the Democratic Party a permanent minority. He talked about the fact that, although poll after poll indicated that the majority of Americans disagreed with Republicans about many issues (abortion, gay rights, peace, education, the environment, etc.), they continued to get elected because they understood two facts:

1. The majority of Americans don't vote. Elections are decided by minorities who care enough to speak up, show up, and give to the causes in which they believe.
2. People know where the Republicans stand on issues. Their strong stand ultimately defines the issue, leaving Democrats to weakly react or respond. "Democrats are

too often considered Republican lite," he said, "and our nation doesn't need two Republican Parties."

Regardless of whether you are a Democrat, Republican, or independent, understanding those two political realities could, and should, completely reshape how we grow our churches. Failing to understand them will lead to our eventual extinction.

Let's apply the first one to church. The Republicans built their political dynasty by appealing relentlessly and obsessively to what they call "their base." In short, they have tailored their campaigns to turning out the conservative and evangelical voters as sure and certain Republican votes. If we can suspend all judgement about their values, we can appreciate that this strategy has been met with great success. They have mobilized a minority of Americans to build a majority of the votes. Whether we like the outcome or not, this kind of targeting has been remarkably effective. Democrats keep pointing to polls that say the majority of Americans agree with their progressive values, but they never seem to realize that polls don't actually vote. The majority of millennials report in survey after survey that they agree with the values of Vintage Churches, but polls don't worship, serve, or give.

In part, the strategy of religious and political conservatives has worked because it has allowed them to tailor their message and focus it relatively tightly. They know they don't really need the support of the majority of Americans. They only need the majority of those who actually show up to vote and that is their target audience. Unfortunately, churches who hold inclusion as a core value seem to have great difficulty appreciating this strategy, let alone applying it. Let me offer a concrete illustration:

Some years ago I led a church growth workshop in Oklahoma City. It was for a congregation that wanted to build their membership and their attendance from 75 on Sunday to around 250. This was a liberal congregation of mostly lesbian and gay people. Although they wanted to be more fully inclusive, they acknowledged that there were a number of other inclusive congregations in Oklahoma City and that their unique offering was their unconditional, and even aggressive, inclusion of lesbian and gay people. We spent a few minutes listing all the reasons why lesbian, gay, bisexual, and transgender people might not attend their church. When the list was fairly comprehensive, I asked them what percentage of the community would be excluded because of at least one of the reasons on the list. The highest guess we got was that probably 50 percent of the LGBT community were not candidates to attend their church. With that in mind, we did a brief calculation:

Population of the city:	610,613
Population of the urban area:	1.3 million
LGBT population (assume five percent):	30,531/65,000
If one percent of LGBT might attend:	305/650

I pointed out that they could write off as much as 99 percent of the LGBT community that lived within the city and 99.6 percent of the community in the metropolitan area, and still exceed their goals. Furthermore, I thought they should acknowledge that they would not reach the majority, and could not serve them if they did, so they should target their ministry to those who needed them and were most receptive to them. The "y'all come" approach taken by most Vintage Churches is ineffectual. We must discern who we are called to be (vision), what we are called to do (mission), and what our guiding core values are. Then we must find our voice and articulate what we have discerned, and we must do it clearly, passionately, creatively, and relentlessly.

You don't need to convince everyone; in fact, you don't really need to convince anyone. All you really need to do is let those who already need you and agree with you find you. Our greatest challenge as progressive, inclusive, and mainline churches, may be to give up the middle of the road where we seem determined to offend no one and therefore end up saying nothing with much resolve or conviction. That was a great realization for them. While it might seem a bit extreme for a church to write off 99 percent of folks, my point was that an attempt to reach 100 percent of the community dooms our efforts to tepid mediocrity. Perhaps it was this principle that Jesus had in mind when he addressed the church of Laodicea in the third chapter of the book of Revelation:

> *I know your works; you are neither cold nor hot. So because you are lukewarm, and neither cold nor hot, I will spit you out of my mouth.*

Jesus had no stomach for the lukewarm, and modern marketers would agree that few Americans find it very appealing today. Vintage Churches must rediscover the voice of our ancestors who spoke loudly, clearly, and consistently for religious freedom at the founding of the country, against slavery when our nation was sorely divided, for the rights of women, against racial segregation, for LGBT equality, for the healing of the earth, for economic equality, etc. We have a long and noble tradition of articulating values and a world vision that most people share, but who would know if we speak so timidly?

Like the Republicans, we don't need to appeal to everyone, and we don't need to appeal to the majority. What we must do is discover to whom our message and ministry do appeal and target our outreach to that group. Then, we need to fail, fail, and fail again to reach them. What we have discovered is that many more of our marketing attempts fail than succeed. That shouldn't surprise us because few churches have the financial resources to do market analysis, test marketing, and mass marketing. Still, it might be some comfort to know that even major corporations with marketing departments larger than our membership produce material that fails much more often than it succeeds. The one principle most marketers urge us to remember is that someone must encounter our name/identity seven or eight times before it really has an impact. You must be prepared to fail and then to try again and again.

Actually, what we have discovered is that much of our effort to reach our "target audience" succeeds more than we know. Our tendency is to send out a postcard or take out an ad and then count the number of new visitors who show up. The truth is few people are sitting around without plans for Sunday just waiting for your postcard to arrive. It may take several weeks before they have a chance to respond, and, by then, they will have forgotten and will need another reminder and then another. Still more likely, the advertisement will have planted a seed that will bear fruit on the day a friend or neighbor invites them to your church, or perhaps the next time there is a crisis in their life or in our nation. On the Sunday after the tragedy of September 11, 2001 we got a true count of how effective our advertising had been when so many first-time visitors attended our church that we had to turn them away because there was not enough room in the building.

Beyond identifying our most likely and logical market, and targeting our outreach efforts to them, there is that second point that the late Senator Kennedy made. He told us that the country didn't need a second Republican party, that it was a mistake for the Democrats to seek to be "Republican lite." That is an important lesson for many churches and even denominations to learn.

The progressive church has been in decline for some time, but not because it is too liberal. It may be because it was not aggressively liberal enough to provide a social alternative. We intellectualized the faith, homogenized worship, and soft-pedaled our core values. It soon became true that the only thing people got out of church was community. As they increasingly found community elsewhere, the church became increasingly irrelevant, not because we had nothing to say, but because we kept saying it so softly or tentatively that they didn't think we had anything to say.

We are so afraid of offending someone that we fail to challenge anyone. We are so terrified that someone will leave that we never do anything to attract anyone new. The Cathedral of Hope grew in one of the most conservative cities in America. Even now the church I pastor is growing in a state that is crimson red. Neither tried to match or adapt to the conservativism of our culture. We did not compromise or cover up our progressive values. In fact, the opposite is true; we seek ways we can voice our differences as loudly as possible. We have a large rainbow banner on our traditional red-brick, white-steepled building not because we are trying to attract

LGBT people, but because it is one way to publically and visibly say that our values are different than many churches and different than the impression that the outside of our building might give. How would people know your church is different from the impression they have about church in general?

Vintage Churches need to rediscover the kind of passion that most often characterizes the fundamentalist and evangelical churches in America. They know how to appeal to the hearts and passion of their congregations. Their worship is filled with fervor and excitement. They care deeply and passionately about the values they espouse. Shouldn't progressives be just as passionate about the core values of our faith? I believe it is not only safe to be fanatically devoted to certain values, but it is also necessary. Let us never be timid in our commitment to values like compassion, inclusion, justice, and peace.

Because we began with a lesson in church growth from a Democrat, perhaps I should pause to quote one of the godfathers of the modern Republican Party. Barry Goldwater said, "Extremism in the defense of liberty is no vice. Moderation in the pursuit of justice is no virtue." In our context, I believe God is calling us to be extremists in defense of the major core values of our faith. It is no virtue for us to be moderate in our pursuit of establishing the realm of God where those virtues are our guiding principles.

By seeking to combine, in equal parts, the intellectual rigor of the liberal church, which values the questions, with the passion and devotion of the conservative church, Vintage Churches can find a formula for growth and vitality even in a more conservative culture. We should be as profoundly devoted to "saving" those "lost souls" from the hells of shame, estrangement, poverty, loneliness, and hopelessness as any fundamentalist church is to saving the lost from the eternal fires of their understanding of hell. We must approach our ministry with no less passion or enthusiasm.

The liberal, progressive, and moderate church must find our voice to speak to people's hearts as effectively as we appeal to their minds. We clearly care, but who would know? In the introduction to his book *The Soul of Politics*, Jim Wallis writes:

> *The world isn't working. Things are unraveling, and most of us know it. Tonight, the urban children of the world's only remaining superpower will go to bed to the sound of gunfire. Bonds of family and community are fraying. Our most basic virtues of civility, responsibility, justice, and integrity seem to be collapsing. We appear to be losing the ethics derived from personal commitment, social purpose, and spiritual meaning. The triumph of materialism is hardly questioned now, in any part of our society. Both domestically and globally, we are divided along the lines of race, ethnicity, class, gender, religion, culture and tribe. Environmental degradation and resource scarcity threaten to explode our divisions into a world of perpetual conflict.*

He wrote those words more than two decades ago, and it seems now that it may have been an optimistic assessment. Our congregations know what is happening in the world around them. What they don't know is what to do about it, what their faith says about it, or what their pastor thinks about it.

Our pews will remain more empty than full unless we can find our prophetic voice and speak clearly and passionately to the multiple crises of our day. We are not required to have all the answers, but, as community leaders, we must at least give voice to the questions and reveal that we are struggling with people to find a way. We are required by our faith to offer a word of hope so convincingly that, even in the midst of a world in despair, the realm of God might break through. Our faith speaks not of escapist optimism, but of God's word of life spoken in a land of crosses and tombs.

We must courageously accept our mantle as prophets of God and call people of faith to transformed values and life-styles. If we refuse we will be relegated to be the priests who offer last rites to our churches and, perhaps, to the faith we love so dearly. Millions of Americans do not wish to be members of the civil Christianity that has come to power in this country. They are desperate for you to articulate an alternative for them.

Chapter Seven
Making "Welcome" an Active Verb

My beloved United Church of Christ declares itself to be "non-creedal," which I appreciate. If we did have a creed, though, it might be the one sentence that is encountered in one way or another in almost every UCC: "No matter who you are, or where you are on life's journey, you are welcome here." It is a beautiful expression of our vision and values as a denomination. The only problem is it isn't true. Frankly, it couldn't be.

You are not welcome in most of our churches if you espouse hateful racist values, or misogynistically insist that God is a white, western male. You probably would not find a warm welcome in most places if one of your values was that God gave mankind (sic) the earth to use and exploit without concern for the future because all Christians are going to be raptured. Our welcome is not unconditional, you see, and it shouldn't be. John Wesley said that, although there must be common core values for community to exist, we should be tolerant of differences on most issues, so, "If your heart is as my heart then take my hand and let us walk together."

Affirming welcome over exclusion is an important message, given the history and practice of what the church too often has done. However, that too often gets lived out as though "welcome" is a passive verb. What we really mean is, you are welcome if you:

- Are persistent enough to find us and come to us.
- Can find a parking place after all of our members have taken most of them.
- Can figure out which door to come in, and how to get from there to the sanctuary through our labyrinth of halls and stairs.
- Know the insider language we use and the secret words to prayers and responses.
- Are extroverted enough to doggedly make your way to the place we all disappear to for bad coffee and cookies after church.
- Brought cash or a checkbook to give the way we always have given.

You get the point. Despite what we claim and what I believe most churches truly desire to be, almost everything we do on Sunday mornings seems designed to put the lie to our creed of welcome. It is at best a passive verb, and we depend on our guests to take us at our word that they are genuinely welcome. We too often follow the "golden rule" when it comes to visitors; that is we do unto them as *we* would have them do unto us. The trouble is we should be doing unto them as *they* would have us do unto them. Their needs/desires are very different than ours, and that is how we should treat them.

The real test of your resolve to offer a radical welcome is to answer, ruthlessly and honestly, this question: "For whom is your worship designed?" Does it serve the needs of those who attend already, or is it carefully crafted so that guests have an optimal experience? To ask that another way, is the congregation oriented to be the Body of Christ—to serve not to be served—or do they see themselves as the consumers of church? It is a pivotal value that determines if a church is oriented toward the future or the past, toward growth or death, inwardly or outwardly, toward themselves or the community.

The only hope ANY church has is that new people will come, come back, and stay, and that they will do so at a rate faster than people are leaving or dying. Despite what we say about our welcoming values, so much of how Vintage Churches behave says that "welcoming the stranger among us" is a peripheral issue. It is not. It is our only hope to survive, let alone thrive, very far into the 21st century. We must make welcome a very active verb and a very high priority as though our life and our guests' depend on it. Ours definitely does, and theirs often might.

Let's explore together, in very practical terms, how this gets lived out.

There must be an authentic change in the DNA of most congregations.

The way we say it around our place is that "the church [members and leaders] must take off our bibs and put on our aprons." That is, everything about us must be reoriented from meeting "our" needs/desires to meeting "theirs." We must stop acting as though we are guests, and become active hosts to any and all who stand in need of the transformational grace that the church supplies. Members must see themselves as the church, the body of the living Christ in the world. Leaders must understand their job to be "equipping the saints" to do just that.

(Ephesians 4:12) Every church I know agrees that their call is to "serve, not to be served," but, almost as unanimously, every church behaves as though the institution should be oriented to meeting their needs and expectations. In order to make the requisite changes for Vintage Churches to thrive again this is the foundational value that must shift.

- At Virginia-Highland Church, we give every new member an apron when they join as a reminder to them, but mostly to the congregation, of our orientation.
- When we welcome visitors/guests we say that the people sitting in the pews around them are the ministers of the church and stand ready to answer their questions or help them in any way. This, too, is designed to remind the members that they are there as hosts, not just to visit with their friends and ignore our guests.
- At the end of worship, I remind the congregation that, although "our worship has ended, now our service begins."
- Every time we have a major decision or make a major change, we remind ourselves that it is not about us; it is about those who need us.

This shift is much more difficult than it seems, but it also is vital to the survival of the church and to those who need what we have to offer. So, as you work on getting your church to take off their bibs and put on their aprons, there are a number of ways that should be expressed if we hope to widen our welcome beyond those who already attend.

Marketing is how you spell evangelism in the 21st century.

Once upon a time every Vintage Church had an evangelism/outreach team or committee. Then we apparently became embarrassed by the fervor of the evangelical church, which seemed to believe that they had to win people to their church lest they go to hell. That was not what we believed, so our value for ecumenism and tolerance became our excuse for making "welcome" more and more of a passive verb. IF you found us and came to us, we would welcome you, but we were too sophisticated to actually invite you. Study after study shows, however, that 80 percent of those who visit a church come because someone has invited them.

Every church needs a communication team whose orientation is to connect with those who do not already attend. From branding to marketing to publicity, every aspect of communication should be crafted with guests in mind. Insider language must be scrubbed completely. Although our members are attached to logos and colors that have served us for decades, we need a team that can design and evaluate our efforts without nostalgia or sentimentality.

A Methodist church I served in the 1980s spent a great deal of money advertising in the local paper. I asked how effective the effort was, but no one seemed to know. One Sunday, I simply asked for a show of hands of those who had found the church through the ad. Of course, not a single hand was raised. Then I asked how many knew what the ad for this week's service had said. Even those who fought to continue advertising could not raise their hands with integrity. Today, no church would think of putting ads in the local paper, though, ironically, that vintage outreach is more effective than it has been in decades for that very reason. Twenty years ago churches used postcards to reach out to their neighborhoods. Then they realized that those cards never even made it into the house, but were tossed out with the catalogues and other junk mail. Today people get most of their junk mail electronically, and postcards and other snail mail have become more effective than they have been in decades, particularly when coupled with effective use of social media.

On Sunday morning, if your congregation would simply "check in" on Facebook and say a word or two about the church or the service the effect could be dramatic. Again, what they say should be oriented to their "friends" who do not attend. The average person has more than 350 friends on Facebook so if 100 church members posted about how much they love their church that would be potentially 35,000 people exposed to a powerful personal witness by someone they know. You do not have to persuade people to go door to door inviting their neighbors, but you do need to reorient them to act like they are hosts telling people about a wonderful party that they love attending.

Look at your website, or, better yet, find some people who don't go to any church to look at your website. Do the same with your Facebook page, and your use of Twitter and Instagram. If those are not evangelism tools your church uses aggressively then your welcome is inauthentic. Ask a team of younger people to help change all that.

Parking is a test and a testimony.

Again, we say that we are a church of radical welcome, but who gets the best parking? Once upon a time, consultants advocated reserving at least 10 percent of your off-street parking for visitors. We tried that for a while, until we noticed that it too often sat empty. People simply did not want to self-identify as being new, lest they be singled out in a way that made them feel uncomfortable.

What worked much better was convincing the congregation to park offsite to leave the closer places for guests. While getting people to make the shift took a while, with persistence and awareness, regular attenders eventually were embarrassed to be seen parking close to the building. It begins with the pastor modeling good behavior by parking far away and walking. Leadership also must help model this behavior. Of course, so many members of Vintage Churches are elderly and cannot walk long distances, so the off-street parking may need to be "reserved" for them, for the differently abled, and for guests. The first test if people have truly "taken off their bibs and put on their aprons" will come on a cold and rainy Sunday morning.

Signage should be clear and consistent.

As someone who visits other churches frequently, it never ceases to amaze me how difficult we make it on guests. I once did a tour of five churches in New England. Heading to the first, my trusty GPS sent me to a church building that had been abandoned and now is a personal residence. A barking dog alerted me to this just before I opened the door and went in.

When I stopped at a local store to ask directions, I was pleased that the first person I asked knew exactly which church I sought. "Drive just east of here about half a mile. You can't miss it. They are the church with all the apple pie signs along the road." Sure enough, that is how I found them. The church was set back from the road, and the very traditional sign with changeable letters was close to the building and parallel to the highway. I was left to wonder how people would find the church after the apple pie fundraiser was over.

The next day, I visited the second church, which Siri found correctly and easily. (Can she find yours? About 20 percent of the time she gets me lost.) I arrived early, parked on the street, and walked around the neighborhood. The signage was similar to the first church, but this building was located close to a main street from which you could see the sign, IF you approached from the right direction. If you came from the other way, good luck.

After a brief walk to assess the neighborhood where the church was located, I went to the front door of the sanctuary to see if it was open. In small town New England the doors often are unlocked. This one was not, and I noticed immediately that there were cobwebs and leaves that said it was unused. I then went looking for how people really entered. I found a large parking lot in back, which I didn't even know existed. Sure enough, the back door was unlocked, and someone soon found me wandering their halls.

I should say that both of these churches are strong and healthy despite inadequate signage, both inside and out. Older Vintage Churches often have been modified and added onto over the years, and sometimes centuries. This often has resulted in a plethora of halls and doors creating a confusing maze for those who get lost wandering through them. Regular attenders almost always use alternative entrances, just as they do at their own homes. Guests, though, almost always start with the front door, even though they must park in back and walk around.

Make sure it is clear how guests find their way, and train all members to act like hosts and guides to those who seem new.

Know your database as well as you know your Bible.

When the late Robert Schuller hired architect Philip Johnson to design the Crystal Cathedral in earthquake-prone Southern California, Johnson asked him how he would ever raise the money for such an expensive project. Schuller's answer in 1979 was, "I will build it with a mailing list." Dr. Schuller once said to me, "Son, if your building ever catches fire leave the offering and everything else but take your mailing list." Today he would have said, "Take your database." That is my advice to you, because churches will be built with good databases.

The future of your congregation, and the congregation of the future, depends more than you can imagine on gently identifying visitors and getting their contact information. You, of course, want to invite them back, but how will you do that if you don't first get their contact information? Vintage Churches are often too passive about this. At a recent arts festival, a company was giving away a new car. In order to win you only needed to register. Now, if contact information is that valuable to a car company, why on earth do churches passively let people come and go without collecting it?

The average church in America has four first-time visitors a week, and if only half of those 208 people returned and joined most churches would double in size. How can you invite them back unless you have their name, address, and/or email address? Your congregation probably has more visitors than you realize because they are not well identified. If not, then that is the first issue that must be addressed. How do you increase those who come into your doors and give your church a chance? We will talk about ideas for that in a later chapter, but, before you attract them, make sure you know how to connect with them when they come.

One year during Lent, one of my daughters attended a church in the community where she went to college. It was a mainline church, and I believe she went for an Ash Wednesday service. When I asked later how it was, she was complimentary but noted that they had not even asked her to register her attendance. At first I was pleased that she had noted that they had neglected something her father relentlessly tries to teach churches to do. Then I realized that she had no way of knowing that. She was expressing the impression that millennials get when the church's message is, "We don't really want to know you." For a generation that sometimes overshares on social media, knows that privacy is an illusion, and connects virtually to the world, if a church does not ask for their information, the welcome is a superficial one. We obviously don't want to get to know them or invite them back, because we haven't even asked for their name.

Millennials will gladly and trustingly give it. Their parents' generation still suffers under the illusion that they have retained some privacy. To get it from them, you need to tell them exactly why you want it and what you are going to do with it. In order to get their grandparents to give you their information you will need to do that and ask them to do it in a way that does not single them out or make them feel conspicuous. Ask everyone in the room to register their attendance, and your guests to be sure to give you their information so you can write to them, welcome them, send them information about the church, and invite them to return. Tell them at the beginning of the service that they are safe and that this is the only thing that will be asked of them. Say it all again at the time of the offering and invite **everyone** to register. The younger the guest the more likely they are to comply, which is good because everyone keeps asking how to get millennials to come back to church.

Once you have made collecting information from guests a priority, it is critical that you have a systematic way to enter that information as soon after church as possible into a responsive database. You then can generate a list and send them an email that very day. A letter with a brochure about the church and perhaps a small gift should be sent on Monday. Every day you delay diminishes the likelihood of their return. We always look new people up on Facebook and note what friends they have who attend church, what they do for a living, where they live, when their birthday is, etc. Older people find this a little creepy, but younger people think it is just common courtesy. If they have put it on Facebook then they already have told you, so why do they need to tell you again? Birthday greetings from all of their "friends" on Facebook is nice, but imagine the impact when the only actual birthday card they receive is from that church they visited a few months ago.

Your database needs to be able to tell you instantly who is there for the first time, and you need a system for responding when a person visits a third time. There is a good possibility that you have identified someone who is ready to connect. Don't passively *hope* they feel welcome; make that welcome active before they drift away feeling unnoticed.

Your database also needs to tell you when a person has missed three Sundays in a row. Pastors almost always will notice when active members go missing for that long. The problem is that new people drop through the cracks much more easily, and, if their absence isn't noticed within a month, they are unlikely to return no matter how often we *say* they are welcome. Most church databases are good at telling you who was there, but the critical information is who has missed.

Because I could not find an affordable database that did what my church needed, I found a team that could design one. That system, which is based on these principles, can be found at AgileChurch.com. In the interest of full disclosure, I should acknowledge that I am a partner in the business. It is just one such tool, though, so find the one that best suits your church's needs and budget. Whatever system you use, find one and learn to use it to make welcome an active verb.

Chapter Eight
From Survive to Thrive

"Failure to thrive" is a medical term that denotes poor weight gain and physical growth failure over an extended period of time in infancy. This term also might be applied to churches that have moved into survival mode.

Like humans, churches that thrive do not all do so in the same way or at the same rate. Vital, healthy, thriving congregations come in many shapes, sizes, and forms. A small congregation in a declining rural community that serves as the connecting force as the area transitions may be thriving as much as a suburban church that is continuously faced with space challenges. Some of the most vibrant congregations in America are located in the decaying inner city where they meet the needs of the poor, homeless, hungry, and afraid. There are congregations who have chosen the road less traveled, which they assume, like Jesus, will lead to their ultimate death, but they have chosen it because they are meeting a need and serving a desperate community. Their heroism should inspire us all by reminding us that the point of our journey through this life by faith is **not** for us to survive. Thriving churches, however, like thriving humans, do share a number of characteristics.

Vitality

Thriving babies are busy babies. They sleep soundly, but when they are awake they are consumed with activities appropriate to their developmental stage. So, too, with thriving churches, there is a palpable energy, vitality, and strength. In the thriving Vintage Churches that it has been my privilege to travel to, worship may be traditional and even liturgical, but it is also is very energetic. There is always a loud conversational buzz before the service as community takes place throughout the sanctuary. During the course of worship, we should laugh, sometimes raucously; weep so openly that each pew should have a small box of Kleenex; applaud vigorously, sometimes the announcements, sometimes the music, sometimes even the sermons. A writer for "D Magazine" who experienced worship at the Cathedral of Hope when I was there attended a service with an overflow crowd, so he was forced to worship from the hinterlands of the fellowship hall. Still, he wrote, "They do worship with a capital W." Even a stranger is aware when they have encountered a thriving church.

That can take many forms. In one of the most secular regions of the country, there is a thriving congregation of mostly youth and college students who gather each night in a gothic building to sing chants and sit in silence. The community of Taizé certainly has provided a model for vital alternative worship. A couple of years ago, I was honored to be the guest preacher at a church in Denver. I was surprised when their pastor told me I didn't need to bring vestments or, for that matter, a clerical collar or tie. Every Sunday, they pack a very traditional building that was once occupied by a United Methodist Church that has since died. They have taken out the organ and now use the space with a band and multimedia screens. The service is filled with energy and with younger people, a group that church seldom attracts in most cities.

While I believe that vital worship is the heart of a thriving church, I must confess that there are congregations who do it in other ways. Some churches pour their best resources into small groups. The cell and celebration model of church became quite popular in the 1990s, and it has proven effective in a culture in which extended family is a memory and authentic community a rarity. Other churches have focused their energy on serving the marginalized and those in need. The smaller congregation I currently serve has made the decision to invest their energy and resources there rather than in worship or programming. There are a few churches that became centers for the arts, and others that distinguished themselves by their children's programs or their programs for seniors.

The point is that a vital church is energetic and passionate about who it has been called to be and what it has been called to do. No church can do all things well, but every thriving church has a ministry or two that defines it and that it wants to share with everyone.

A baby takes hold of your finger and will not let go. "What a strong grip she has," you might say. So, too, thriving churches have a strong grip on the reality of their situation. They know their future as well as their past. They have assessed their strengths and decided how to best utilize them in contributing to God's realm coming on earth as it is in heaven.

Healthy DNA

Thriving babies are genetically healthy. So, too, healthy, vital faith communities pay attention to their DNA. In their book *Cracking Your Congregation's Code: Mapping Your Spiritual DNA to Create Your Future*, Robert Norton and Richard Southern write:

> *There's more to your congregation than meets the eye. Just as the human organism inherits certain genetic traits, characteristics, and dispositions that in combination make up the whole person, so your congregation has a complex inheritance. Many factors, including denominational, liturgical, and cultural inheritance, go into making it what it is. Author Ken Wilber says that "to understand the whole, it is necessary to understand the parts. To understand the parts, it is necessary to understand the whole."*

Consultant and author Thomas Bandy introduced me to the idea of churches having their own DNA and the importance of each congregation discerning just what theirs really is. Bandy identifies three major areas in the life of a church and 11 subsystems of congregational life. They are:

- **Foundational**
    - Genetic Code: the identity of the church
    - Core Leadership: the seriousness for mission in the church
    - Organization: the structure of the church for mission

- **Functional**
  - Changing Lives: how people experience God in the church
  - Growing Christians: how people grow in relationship to Jesus
  - Discerning Call: how people discover their place in God's plan
  - Equipping Disciples: how people are trained for ministries
  - Deploying Servants: how people are sent and supported in the world
- **Formal**
  - Property: the location, facility and technology
  - Finance: stewardship, budget, debt-management
  - Communication: information, marketing, advertising

As a consultant, Bandy has a series of questions in relation to each of the 11 sub-systems. He also asks for:

1. Community demographic data
2. A leadership readiness survey completed by the staff and church board
3. A church stress test completed by the worshipping congregation, staff, and church board

The differences in perception can be revealing, and the gaps in the data can be significant indicators. He notes that thriving churches always are looking for extra help. This is a post-modern approach. The modern approach assumes if you are healthy you do not need help. Coaching help, not fix-it help, is the post-modern approach. Thriving churches look for ways to connect with other churches, denominational programs, and/or parachurch organizations in a way that supports continued learning and development.

He talks about **ministry mapping**, not strategic planning. Strategic planning, which he says is dying, is long distance, linear, assumes a uniform context, emphasizes technicians, property, and programs, and has a chain of command. Mission mapping is micro-macro in approach, explorational, opportunistic, based on the DNA of the organization, and done in teams. According to Bandy, effective teams have a mission attitude, a work ethic, a variable plan, and a winning faith. Worship reinforces the congregational DNA.

This synopsis of his work doesn't do justice to the insights he offers. Perhaps the greatest contribution that he and his colleague Bill Easum make is to challenge us to think of our congregations in new ways. The healthcare of a non-thriving infant is quite different if the challenge is genetic rather than nutritional. So, too, with our churches.

Relational

Numerous studies have been done that connect an infant's failure to thrive with touch deprivation. Children in Russian and Eastern Bloc countries during the Cold War often displayed symptoms of marasmus (severe undernourishment) even though they were well fed and kept in a sterile environment. It was later discovered that their disease was rooted completely in the fact that infants need affection and physical touch almost as much as they need nutrition.

This seems an important lesson for liberal and progressive churches. People need to be touched as much as they need to be informed. Our worship, sermons, and programs should be shaped to touch people and connect them to God and one another as much as to educate them and inform them about God. We live in a day when people hunger much more for an encounter with God than they do for information about God. Our theological education serves us only in as much as it equips us to help our congregants join hands with one another, the world, and the Ultimate.

Theologian Dr. Leonard Sweet, talking about the shift from a modern to post-modern world, said, "Someday I will hold up my Bible before a congregation, shake it, and yell at the top of my lungs, 'This is not a book about propositions and programs and principles. This is a book about relationships.'" He uses the acronym EPIC—Experiential, Participatory, Image rich, and Connected—to describe how the church must function in a post-modern world. In his book *Postmodern Pilgrims*, Dr. Sweet makes a strong case for the shifts that our churches must make if we are going to be relevant to the lives of those growing up on Starbucks and eBay.

An infant will not thrive no matter how many times a parent tells them they love them. Babies must be touched, caressed, and held, and so must our congregations. Babies must be nourished and have their needs met, and so must our congregations. This is not to say that we need to treat church members like babies; it simply is to say that we must treat them like humans, humans living in the 21st century. They are busy, hurting people who don't have time to participate in activities that do not add value to their lives. Among the deepest needs modern Americans have are community, connection, and contact with one another and, we believe, with God. This is exactly what the church has to offer. So why aren't our churches thriving? In part it is because we still are functioning within a 20th-century paradigm.

Please do not hear this as advocating that the only way the church can thrive is to discard or disregard the needs of older generations. The truth is, though, as our older members face the end of their lives they would much rather have a hand to hold than theology to learn. Unlike their parents and grand-parents, this generation of seniors is the first in history to face the ends of their lives NOT surrounded by extended family members. Their children, grandchildren, nieces, and nephews are scattered to the four winds. The church has the perfect opportunity to be their extended family and truly to be there for them. We must recognize this connectional need and meet it in such a way that the succeeding generations will recognize that church is still the place where they can belong from birth to death.

The Cathedral of Hope suffered greatly during the AIDS crisis. Leader after leader was stricken and died. Six of the 10 people who served on the pulpit search committee that called me to be their pastor were dead before I celebrated my seventh anniversary. The church itself easily could have died. Many predominantly lesbian, gay, bisexual, and transgender churches did. Our congregation, however, rose up to care for the sick and dying so aggressively that every funeral and memorial became an evangelism event. People would rise to talk about the deceased, but, inevitably, they also would talk about the members of our congregation who had been with him until the end. They would bear witness to the caring grace of a place called Hope, and people at the service who hadn't been inside a church in years decided to give it another try. The year when we read more than 180 names on All Saints Sunday, we also received more than 300 new members.

Nourishment

Like me, you probably grew up going to Sunday school. You probably learned things there like how many books there are in the Bible and the names of the four Gospels. There have been a number of articles about the appalling biblical illiteracy that exists in our world today. Author and environmental activist Bill McKibben wrote a great article for "Harper's Magazine" entitled "The Christian Paradox" in which he observed:

> *Only 40 percent of Americans can name more than four of the Ten Commandments, and a scant half can cite any of the four authors of the Gospels. Twelve percent believe Joan of Arc was Noah's wife. This failure to recall the specifics of our Christian heritage may be further evidence of our nation's educational decline, but it probably doesn't matter all that much in spiritual or political terms. Here is a statistic that does matter: Three quarters of Americans believe the Bible teaches that "God helps those who help themselves." That is, three out of four Americans believe that this uber-American idea, a notion at the core of our current individualist politics and culture, which was in fact uttered by Ben Franklin, actually appears in Holy Scripture. The thing is, not only is Franklin's wisdom not biblical; it's counter-biblical. Few ideas could be*

further from the gospel message, with its radical summons to love of neighbor. On this essential matter, most Americans—most American Christians—are simply wrong, as if 75 percent of American scientists believed that Newton proved gravity causes apples to fly up.

Asking Christians what Christ taught isn't a trick. It is important that we educate people to carry on the faith. I have come to believe, however, that people know what is important to them, what helps them get through each day, what improves their life, and what might be helpful to them or their families. The average American's appalling religious education is testimony to the fact that we have not convinced them that what we have to offer can help their daily life and nourish their souls.

My life partner since 1980 is a certified wine educator. There are a variety of ways to teach people more about wine, and there are a number of reasons why wine classes are so popular these days. One reason, of course, is that people enjoy learning. If that was the primary motivation, though, he would be out of business pretty fast. Most people who take these classes want to know more about wine so they won't be embarrassed when ordering wine in a restaurant or by serving the "wrong wine" for dinner. Bill recognized early on that most of his students didn't really want to know the various regions in which certain grapes are grown, or the soil acidity or climate contrasts that produce certain varietals. He had to know all of these things because he is a professional. He also had to learn them to graduate. Now his library is full of books he never uses, and his head is full of information that no one really cares about. He could impose this information on his classes because he finds it fascinating or because he thinks it is important. Ultimately, though, his philosophy is to let people taste wines paired with the various foods they might order or serve so they will know what wine enhances their dining experience. Let those who have ears hear ...

Ultimately, we must offer our members the information that will enhance their spiritual lives. We must help them learn spiritual principles for living their lives. When we do this they will come to value the source of this information: the church, the Bible, theology, etc. I often am asked by members which version of the Bible they should buy. It is a question that warms any pastor's heart because it signifies a spiritual hunger. I have taken to suggesting that, rather than starting with a 2,000-year-old text, they might read a couple of books about the Bible. I have discovered that people who first read, for example, Marcus Borg's *Reading the Bible Again for the First Time* are far more likely to make it past Genesis chapter one.

• • •

Churches thrive in a variety of ways. I probably have carried the analogy of infants thriving too far already, but let me offer one last parallel. A thriving infant brings beauty to the entire world. None of us are so cynical that we can resist smiling back into the face of a happy, healthy cooing baby. Having been a pastor for decades to a community that sees the church as the enemy of its civil rights and happiness, I am very conscious of how the community responds to our churches. Do they see us as an asset to the common life of the neighborhood, town, or city in which we are located? Is it a place to which they would send their children and take their friends, and suggest to new neighbors? Do they think we are a thriving, vibrant, relevant place where people go to experience God and join community? Or do they see us as a place where something happens on Sunday mornings, but they haven't a clue what? Worse yet, perhaps they don't even see us at all because we are so irrelevant to their lives. They would never think to cross our thresholds, even in a time of crisis. There are lots of ways for a church to thrive, but, perhaps, a church that doesn't want to find at least one way ought to turn their facility into a theater or community center. At least, then, someone's needs will be met there.

Chapter Nine
Liberating Generosity

Along with diminishing membership and attendance, the Vintage Church also has suffered diminished giving. Many churches survive only because of their endowments, and those are being whittled away in many places. Other congregations like mine at Virginia-Highland Church survived only by renting much of their building. Neither of these things are bad; in fact, even though we no longer need rent to survive, I'm of the opinion that using a building the size or ours only on Sundays, or even primarily on Sundays, is bad stewardship of God's resources. Although we are not quite there yet, my goal is to have our giving meet all the needs of the church and to use other income like rent to do service projects and outreach ministry that might not otherwise be possible for a church our size. We launched a homeless ministry that we hope will grow beyond our capacity to fund it alone. We don't know where the funding will come from when it outgrows what we can do, but we launched it with the plan that it will outgrow us eventually if we succeed.

All of that is to say that funding sources like grants, rent, and endowments are great tools by which the church can, and should, do an abundance of ministry. It is my firm belief, however, that the congregation's giving should meet the congregation's needs. There are many ways a church can grow the generosity of the congregation, but letting them be dependent on other forms of income is not one of them.

I should confess that, on any given day, I change my mind about why church leaders avoid, or at least flinch when it comes to, teaching and preaching about money. Some days I think it is because we still haven't made peace with our own money issues. Seminary sure doesn't teach you how to have a healthy relationship with the most powerful force in our society. My parents treated money a lot like sex: it was something taken care of behind closed doors and not in front of the kids. We always sensed when there was something wrong in that area, but no one ever sat me down and had a father/mother-to-son dollars-and-cents talk. Most of us learned what we knew about money "on the street" or by trial and error.

When my partner and I became a couple in 1980 money was the area where our values conflicted the most. We never really fought about it, but it took a lot of late night talking to uncover the roots of our values and why we dealt with money the way that we did. Fortunately, when it came to church, my family lived out of a sense of almost illogical generosity. His family were dutiful Baptists, so, from day one, there was no conflict about giving a generous proportion to the church. Through the years, as our lives became more financially secure, we came to realize that we could afford to give considerably more than the standard 10 percent. During the times when we struggled to make ends meet, we managed to look up and see that much of the world around us didn't even have ends. To that, another of Jesus' pithy sayings seemed to speak: "To whom much is given, much is expected." Essentially, our conscience wouldn't allow us to enjoy all we had until we felt we were doing as much as possible to help others have more.

We were the fortunate ones. Both of our families seemed to have reasonably healthy relationships with money, and we inherited this relationship. We can take no credit for that, and didn't even recognize it for many years. Through the years, in the context of both pastoral counseling and friendships, I became painfully aware that money is a significant source of conflict in relationships. So, too, in my consulting work with churches, I have come to realize that, if a pastor has been in a church more than four years and the church is having financial conflicts or a shortfall, there is a good chance that the pastor and his/her family have personal money issues.

Once upon a time, I naively assumed that all pastors and church leaders gave generously. Over the years, though, I have found that the pastors on my own staff often were the best paid but the least generous staff leaders. In our system, the board of directors or parish council has the responsibility of financial oversight, but all too often they didn't assume personal responsibility.

All of this may seem like I am meddling in personal issues; however, it has been a consistent truth that resolving a church's financial challenges must begin with helping leadership resolve theirs. In some cases, pastors have missed the reality that, despite their best efforts, a congregation always knows what a pastor does or does not give. Modeling generosity is a crucial foundation for faithful stewardship, and failure to do so provides many the excuse they need to avoid their own responsibilities. Why should they sacrifice to advance the Realm of God financially if their spiritual leader does not do so? We cannot speak of stewardship with conviction unless we also speak with integrity. We cannot effectively teach that which we do not really know or truly believe.

Perhaps there is a more metaphysical reality here. There is one scripture about which I am a fundamentalist, because I am convinced it is one of the fundamental laws of the universe: "What we sow we also reap." If we who would lead are conflicted about money and not able to live with integrity, generosity, and gratitude, we unconsciously sow those very seeds in the souls of our congregations. Only the generous person can speak of generosity without a catch in their throat.

The other reason that congregational leaders avoid speaking directly and effectively about money is that religious hucksters have given all of us a bad reputation. Sinclair Lewis' 1927 novel *Elmer Gantry*, and the 1960 movie based upon it, haunt us all. More contemporaneously were the televangelists and their scandals and, now, those preachers touting the "Prosperity Gospel." Who can blame us for not wanting to be associated with any of them? At the risk of rubbing salt in the wounds I already have inflicted, let me add that our fears of appearing to channel a televangelist are greatly magnified if our own consciences are not clear. This guilt/shame is compounded by the fact that almost every pastor's livelihood is funded by the giving of our members. Let's simply acknowledge that this creates a nearly intolerable conflict of interest. Even that, however, does not excuse us of our responsibility to be true to the full message of the Gospel.

All of these seem to be principal reasons why we don't do an adequate job of teaching people how to be good stewards of their resources. Let me suggest two very basic reasons we must overcome these encumbrances and become effective spiritual leaders in this area.

First, it is a prominent, perhaps dominant, spiritual truth taught in the Bible. We liberals are as guilty as fundamentalists of seeing what we are looking for when we read the Bible, yet a naïve reading of the Gospels probably would shock us in this area. Jesus talks about money, materialism, possessions, and stewardship more than all other issues combined; in fact, some say more than all other subjects combined. Jesus didn't talk about money as a fundraising technique, but as a core principle of life. This would be a strong argument for separating our stewardship lessons from our pledge campaigns. Jesus told parables of stewardship as a matter of course in talking about how we live our lives. We who are faithful to the assigned lessons of the lectionary cannot avoid talking about money.

From John 3:16's message of God's giving, to the self-giving kenosis of Jesus in Philippians, giving is such a core message of Christianity that I would argue that only the generous can be true disciples of Jesus.

The other reason I believe it is critical that we not neglect our responsibility in this area is that nothing is more damaging to our people than the hold materialism has on our souls. Generosity is the only antidote.

It is the lesson Jesus tried repeatedly to teach, but the multi-billion marketing industry has not only completely drowned out that message, but has hijacked Jesus for their merchandising purposes. A few years ago, when marketers at General Motors used the old Shaker tune "'Tis a Gift to be Simple" to sell one of its highest priced vehicles, I knew we were in a struggle to the death for the souls of our people. As a contemporary spiritual leader, you don't need me to tell you how pervasive this disease is or the extent of its devastation. I'm sure you have quoted the statistics in your own lessons.

In his book *The Crisis in the Church: Spiritual Malaise and Fiscal Woe*, sociologist Robert Wuthnow grieves for the lack of economic and stewardship visions in the church and for its failure of spirit. He places much of the responsibility at the feet of pastors.

A decade ago, Donald A. Luidens, who was then professor of sociology at Hope College in Holland, Michigan, wrote an excellent analysis of Wuthnow's work in "Christian Century":

> *Wuthnow describes the churches' "fiscal woes" in great detail. He suggests, however, that they are mere symptoms of the real issue, which "is a spiritual crisis [that] derives from the very soul of the church. The problem lies less in parishioners' pocketbooks than in their hearts and less in churches' budgets than in clergy's understanding of the needs and desires of their members' lives." Sadly, many clergy simply don't understand that the core problem is a "spiritual malaise." The carrier of that disease is middle-class culture. The middle-class ethos, the cultural ecology within which the church exists, is replete with themes that have stifled parishioners' spirit. As members of the middle class themselves, clergy are blind to the cultural motifs that threaten their parishioners' well-being and the churches' survival.*

There is a grave danger in the fact that we are inevitably infected by the same disease that afflicts the overwhelming majority of our congregations, and we, therefore, don't feel the sense of urgency to offer a cure. Like most middle-class people, we, too, feel overwhelmed by demands. At work, at leisure, or at home, people barely can contend with all that is expected of them. From the proverbial "soccer moms," to the overextended professionals and managers, and blue- and white-collar workers facing the abyss of unemployment, middle-class Americans are riven by angst over what lies before them and by guilt over what they have left undone.

Wuthnow goes on describing their dilemma and ours:

> *They can't even talk about their predicament, since financial matters are considered private, not to be spoken of even to one's pastor or fellow parishioners. Christians lack an effective vocabulary for discussing with each other the economic and financial pressures on their lives. Lacking a theological framework, clergy too easily lapse into the saccharin reassurances of a gospel of happiness, which stresses health and wealth and simplistically equates faithful living with economic success and personal happiness. Or they proclaim a message of passive dependence—"God will provide"—which fosters complacency and inaction. Neither the gospel of happiness nor the gospel of dependence offers practical hope.*

Church leaders' ignorance and anxieties about the mechanics of the economy confound these problems. Wuthnow points out that many clergy are highly suspicious of the "secular" world of work. To the many who have never been employed outside the church, the world of secular employment is foreign, perhaps hostile, territory. Second-career pastors have generally felt themselves "called out" of the secular workforce. Consequently, they too often do not see the work environment in positive theological terms. Clergy's suspicions of the work world have been reinforced by their counseling of parishioners who have been wounded by overwork, unemployment, absentee parenthood, or other malignancies related to work.

Wuthnow points out that the vast majority of Americans love their jobs and find their identity inextricably wrapped up in them. Their occupations are where their hearts find a home, a place of considerable reward and fulfillment, a place begging for theological definition. Most people are so tied to their occupations that their fear of losing their jobs has as much to do with its threat to their identities as with the loss of income. Because clergy do not fully recognize this reality, Wuthnow argues, they do not realize the importance of thinking theologically about work. Wuthnow wants the church to reclaim the concept of vocation as it applies to the work life of each Christian. Since clergy regularly refer to their own "calling," they should readily understand vocation's potential value to the identity—both secular and sacred—of their parishioners.

This issue is certainly worthy of our examination and of an honest response of self-examination. The focus of this chapter primarily has been that we who would dare to lead the people of God must begin that journey at the center of our own being. The issue of money and stewardship is no different. In fact, if we take the words of Jesus with which we began this chapter seriously and personally, this is the primary issue about which we must ruthlessly examine our own hearts. Then, from true wisdom, and with humility and integrity, we can speak of spiritual principles to our fellow strugglers.

It now feels somewhat pedestrian to move to some of the practical issues that might strengthen the financial state of our congregations, yet it is probably what you hoped I would do all along …

When I arrived at the Cathedral of Hope in 1987 the church was on the verge of bankruptcy. It was unable to pay its bills or even the moving expenses of its new pastor. Although I took a 25 percent cut in pay, they were occasionally unable to pay my full salary. With balloon notes coming due on the two buildings on their campus, they faced the distinct possibility of homelessness. The economy of Texas in the late 1980s neared depression levels, with the collapse of the savings and loan, real estate, and oil and gas industries. Unemployment was high, and almost all of the significant donors in the church were bankrupt or dying. Even writing this description makes me wonder what on earth I was thinking by going there.

With no endowments and few significant donors, 20 years after my arrival, their consolidated offerings reached $5 million, and they gave away more than $1.3 million in services and assistance to the poor beyond our church every year. The social and economic circumstances today are substantially different, and, when I left, we had many more members. What might be helpful, then, is to share some of the principles that contributed to that transformation, and some of the practical lessons I had to learn the hard way.

First, it was necessary to create an atmosphere of hope. No one invests in a sinking ship. If there is a general sense that failure is inevitable then it is unreasonable to expect generosity.

On the other hand, I have seen churches that decided they ultimately would close find a renewed sense of meaning and purpose in how they faithfully faced that final time. Having worked with many who were dying, most of us know that there often is a joy that goes far beyond the immediate circumstances. If that is not the work of our faith then what do we mean by resurrection?

In the Cathedral's case, hope began to break forth when we simply painted walls that had been water stained for too long. The next step was to remind a congregation that was literally dying of AIDS that it still had much to give. Turning inward and focusing on self-care had very nearly proven fatal. Mobilizing the congregation to serve others in need was an instrument of rebirth. While many lesbian, gay, bisexual, and transgender congregations were decimated by the AIDS crisis, ours experienced a genuine revival in every sense of that word.

Given the circumstances of the economy, and the staggering burden of our death rate and health crisis, it would have been easy to slip into a sense of scarcity. While I find the current "Prosperity Gospel" to be a clear violation of the most sacred teachings of Jesus, I do understand why it has found a hold in many minority and impoverished communities. When you are surrounded by, and confronted with, so many economic needs, it is easy to assume that there simply is not enough to go around.

That is not true. Today, more than any time in human history, we have enough. There is enough to eliminate hunger and poverty and much of the suffering they bring. The problem is not a scarcity of resources, but of will. Clearly, our job as spiritual leaders is to convince our fellow disciples that we are responsible for helping our nation find the will. In some cases, it must begin by convincing our congregations that the resources are available for them to fulfill their vision.

In her book *Raising More Money*, Terry Axelrod, a professional fundraiser and social worker, tells the story of a friend, a successful employee of Microsoft, who attended a fundraiser for an organization in which he deeply believed:

> *You know how much I love Organization X. They do incredible work internationally to end poverty and hunger. Their overhead is under two percent. Their total budget for the year, to do all they do, is only one million dollars.*
>
> *Last night was their annual fund-raising dinner here in Seattle. Their goal was to raise $100,000, or 10 percent of their whole budget. They succeeded. They were ecstatic.*
>
> *I'm still upset about it ... that they were happy to settle for so little. I love that organization. If they had even thought to ask me, I'd have funded their whole budget for the year.*
>
> *Then I think to myself ... I'm sitting here right now on the Microsoft campus, looking out at all these people. So many of these people could have funded this organization several times over, or for that matter, funded **their** favorite charity many times over or fully funded that organization's endowment. But no one's asking us!*

Some years ago, when we announced our campaign to build a new facility, Pat Robertson's news program on the Christian Broadcasting Network reported our intentions. They ended their report with a snide remark about the fact that, at the time, we did not have the money even to complete the architectural designs. That Sunday, as we launched our capital campaign, I showed a video clip of that taunt. Then turned to the congregation and said, "They are wrong about that. We **do** have the money to complete the design. We just haven't collected it yet, but we are going to change that right now." That morning, hundreds of people came forward and gave more than enough money to pay the architectural fees and to launch our capital campaign with which to begin construction.

Giving a congregation a sense of hope that overcomes attitudes of fear and lack and scarcity is just the beginning. Ultimately, the leaders of the church must have the courage to ask people to give their money to our mission. This is all too often where we pastors fail. We never "close the sale." How often have we taught people the principles of living with generosity and gratitude only to watch them practice those principles with their alma mater, the local symphony, or some other charity? The epistle of James rebukes us for that, saying, "You have not because you ask not." Sisters and brothers, "ask" is not a four-letter word. Millard Fuller, the founder and leader of Habitat for Humanity, likes to say, "I have tried raising money by asking for it and by not asking for it, and I always got more by asking for it."

While there are many ways to fund a church, almost all of them come down to asking people for money. As obvious as that may seem, it apparently is not so evident to everyone. In a 1995 study 60 percent of Americans reported that they had been asked to give money; today fewer than 40 percent report that they have been asked by a church or nonprofit to give money.

That decline means that millions of dollars simply were not given last year because no one asked for it.

Of all the money given away in this country 90 percent comes from individuals; 82 percent of that comes from families who earned $60,000 or less. Many churches and charities focus on the wealthy, but 78 percent of the under-asked say yes, which is six times as often as the wealthy say yes when asked. Of course, the wealthy get asked much more often, and they have on hand their excuses for not giving. They are excuses, because those who make more than $250,000 a year give away less than 1 percent of their income, while those who earn less than $15,000 give 4 percent of their income.

So, while we could explore how you raise money from large donors, and there is certainly a science to that, ultimately, more than three-quarters of the money you raise will come from middle-class philanthropists. As good, progressive people, we have some guilt about the fact that those who can "least afford" to give away money will be funding our congregations. However, that attitude is really disrespectful to those who believe they have something to give. Most of them manage to feed themselves and their families and don't need us to give them free spiritual food any more than they need the local café to give them free meals. Their self-respect requires them to pay their way, and, to them, anything less would be theft.

In conclusion, let me list some of the very practical things we can do to help fund the ministry to which God has called us:

Have a Pledge Drive

I hate it; you hate it; they hate it. Still, it works. People who pledge give an average of three times more money than those who don't. If you decide not to ask for pledges then you have to spend more time fundraising in other ways, or reduce the amount of money you can raise. Perhaps a better strategy might be to reframe our annual campaigns.

Like many pastors, I used to prefer fall stewardship campaigns connected to the next year's budget. Then, one year, our calendar did not allow for that. Instead, we made it a part of our challenge to Lenten discipline. We asked people to try tithing (10 percent) for 40 days or, at the very least, to enter into a financial covenant as a part of their Lenten observance. This spiritual practice was coupled with a call to observe other classic disciplines of the church, as well as an "Experiment in Practicing Christianity." People were told that if they were faithful and the practices did not enrich their lives they could quit after Easter, no questions asked. Everyone was asked to sign a pledge of faithfulness.

We were staggered to find that, for the first time, spring was our strongest season in every measurable way. After that, the congregation practiced Lent with great devotion. I now like to call people in our membership classes "Covenant Keepers," and we ask them to make six covenants at their confirmation to uphold the church with their prayers, presence, gifts, services, witness, and to grow as a disciple of Jesus. Each Lent we try to find ways to remind our members of the covenant they made and to call them to renew those covenants **in writing**.

Rather than making the pledge drive a means of haranguing people into underwriting the budget, why not find new and creative ways to incorporate it into a campaign to total spiritual renewal? Written pledges of prayer, service, devotion, generosity, etc. are all powerful. Why should we be more reluctant to ask people to sign a covenant than the local gym? We, too, are working to help people to be more disciplined and healthy.

Create a year-round stewardship plan and stick to it. If you don't have a written plan, it's not going to happen. It should include how generosity will be taught in every setting, small group, and class; what communication methods are available and how they will be used; how each element fits within the church calendar; who is responsible for specific tasks along with due dates; who will respond to donors when they have questions, donate, or promise to donate; and how success will be evaluated or measured.

The budget, or, perhaps, "goals for ministry," should be communicated in terms of how ministry expresses the vision and values of the church and what could be accomplished to help achieve the mission if everyone is more generous. No one is inspired by an accounting spreadsheet, yet that is how most churches present financial needs. Tell the story of what was done and paint a picture of what you could do and let the accountants in the congregation read their figures to their heart's content. There is nothing to hide, but the truth is all those dry numbers end up hiding the Truth.

Every appeal for financial support should begin with the financial commitment of leaders and clergy. It's important for leaders to model generous behavior if you ever expect the congregation to be generous. These same leaders also should have a role in communicating the needs of the church to small groups, individuals, and key donors. Create a leadership covenant that models the kind of ideal behavior toward which everyone should strive. In our church, leaders are asked to tithe, pray daily for their pastor and fellow leaders, deal directly with disagreements or conflict, and fully keep their membership vows year-around, not just during Lent.

Most churches have some sort of annual appeal for funding, but we sometimes do an inadequate job of following up with the results of the congregation's generosity. It's sometimes difficult to toot our own horn, but donors want to know that their gifts had an impact. Show them how their gifts are changing the world, and you will inspire a lifelong giver. Consistently celebrate ministry successes and find multiple ways to show how lives are being changed through the work of the church.

Exploit the Shift from Giving to Spending

My parents give money to their church. They make a pledge every year, and they write a check and drop it in the plate when it passes every Sunday. God love them because they are a dying breed. There are fewer and fewer pure givers in America, yet charitable giving actually has increased most of the past decade. How can that be?

Many pastors that I talk to see news reports about the increase in charitable giving and shake their heads because that certainly has not been their personal experience. That is true with many charities as well. Most of the executive directors I know have to deal with budget shortfalls. The breakdown seems to be that giving statistics are distorted because people have been responding generously to specific crises. Beginning with September 11, 2001, Americans have responded to disasters like tsunamis and hurricanes, but have not underwritten the operating costs of the churches and organizations that simply have sought to serve everyday needs.

The truth is, when it comes to charities and churches, Americans are increasingly **spenders** not **givers**. Ask people to buy new hymnals or playground equipment and the money arrives in buckets, but the offering plate returns increasingly empty. Now, we have two options here. We can rail against this trend and try to hold back the tide, or we can figure out new ways to let this new reality fund the work of God.

Let me offer a couple of examples of how we have tried to ride this wave rather than resist it. At the Cathedral of Hope, we created a program called "Child of Hope" through which the congregation serves children in need, including their own children and youth. Each year they receive a second offering during Advent and on Christmas Eve, and also give members the opportunity to give a donation to Child of Hope in honor of their family and friends rather than simply buying another gift that someone really doesn't need. If the donor gives an address, the honoree receives an acknowledgement card as their Christmas gift.

This program has raised thousands of dollars. The danger with programs like this, of course, is that we might divert money from the general fund to a designated fund that can be used only for the purpose for which it was solicited. To mitigate that we use an appropriate portion of the money raised to pay the salaries of the staff who manage the ministry and disperse the services. Through a wide variety of programs like this, the Cathedral of Hope raised more money and was able to lower the general fund budget without lowering services or reducing staff.

A few years ago, the Internal Revenue Service ruled that donations that are designated by the donor are not tax-deductible. Their explanation was that the donor was actually **spending** money not **giving** money. Donations are only tax-deductible if the institution is free to determine how the money is to be spent. Of course, money that churches solicit for a specific purpose is tax deductible. However, if a donor simply decides to give money for a specific purpose because it was something they wanted, rather than something for which the church asked, then the donor is spending money not giving it. I have found this IRS ruling useful in helping donors understand the difference between spending and giving. Still, it is the cultural reality in which we must raise money today.

Increase Your Use of Technology

Like most churches, mine receives less and less money in the offering plate each year, yet our budget and income continue to grow. Every month the amount of money donated electronically through our website, by credit card, and automatic withdrawals increases. Nearly 50 percent of our donations are given automatically. By using a credit card or authorizing an automatic deduction from their checking account members contribute whether or not they attend. People who move away often continue giving until they find a new church home.

Older members in long-established congregations attend church with great regularity. The average age of our congregation is almost 20 years younger than a typical mainline church. Because of that demographic, our people tend to attend much less often. Given the irregularity with which even our most dedicated members attend, the auto-givers sustain the church in a critical way. By and large, the generation that has been acculturated to spend rather than give contribute only when present. For them, attending and giving once a month qualifies as active. Usually, when they sign up for auto-giving, it is at the rate at which they give when they attend. The net result is that their annual giving is substantially increased.

More and more churches are installing giving kiosks where people who arrive at church without cash or checkbook can simply and quickly swipe their credit or debit card and make a contribution. We have been told for many years that we are moving to a cashless society. Today, that is true almost everywhere but the church. Even vending machines and parking meters have had to adapt to this reality. The more quickly the church does as well the better.

At the Cathedral of Hope we used a service by which every member of the church was mailed giving envelopes monthly. The cost of this is much less than we would have to pay just for postage. We found doing so increased our giving by about 15 percent, and every person gets at least one mailing from the church every month. This company also mails a series of cards to automatic givers that they can drop in the offering plate when it passes. This way it doesn't appear to their peers that they don't give. The cards are brightly colored and thus, as they fill the offering plate as it passed down the pew, they also serve as a great marketing tool for our auto-giving program.

At Virginia-Highland Church we do not use such a service, but we have placed laminated auto-giving cards in the pew racks. They include a QR (quick response) code that can be scanned by a smartphone, taking the congregant to the giving page on our website. The same QR code is printed on the back of the bulletin.

Your Bible and Your Database

Every fundraising professional in your city will tell you that raising money is almost 100 percent about relationships. Frequently, leaders become renowned for the fact that they write notes to so many people. It is an amazing discipline to write two or three thank you notes a day. While emails are the modern equivalent, they still have not replaced the value of a handwritten note. Developing relationships with present and future donors is critical to the long-term financial health of any church or nonprofit.

When I arrived in Dallas we took Polaroid pictures of every person who attended membership class. I'd walk around for days with those pictures memorizing every name and any other information we might have. Still today, I know the names of every one of the first 1,000 members. Then my RAM got full, or something. Today I have a hard time remembering the names of my friends. While you may not have 1,000 people to get to know, you should act as if you do, because if you remain in a community very long you soon will.

Before a fundraiser approaches a donor they learn absolutely everything they can about them. They want to know their giving history, what they like, who they are related to, how they vote, where they like to eat, what their pets' names are, and any other information that might possibly be helpful in getting the person to donate. How much more should that be true of pastors? None of our memories are sufficient. We must keep very good notes of phone calls and conversations.

We also need to collect every email address and mailing address we possibly can. If you have ever tried to buy a mailing list you quickly discovered just how valuable that information is to those raising money. There are many apps available that are free and can connect you to people via their social media accounts. A good database will do that and help you keep up with birthdays so you can send "cards" to people on their special day.

In my own theological framework, the Bible is not the Word of God, but God often does speak to me through it. In those moments, it becomes God's word. So, too, recordkeeping is not a relationship and will not raise you any money, but diligence in this regard can enhance your relationships and become the source of funding.

Create an Effective Case Statement

Before launching any capital campaign a professional will ask the organization to create a case statement. That is probably a good exercise for anyone. While various people have definitions for what makes a good case statement, this is what I have in mind. In essence, it is a "data dump" that creates a central source for your mission, vision, passion, direction, strategy, and unique philosophy. There is no need to state the obvious or to define the word "church," but this is a good place to state clearly how your church is unique, special, needed. You are making a case for your existence and funding. Why should I give you my hard-earned money?

In my opinion, the length really doesn't matter. It probably should be 15-30 pages long. You will never publish it or use it in its total form, but from it every piece of information about your church should be drawn. You should be able to hand it to a total stranger to create your website and s/he should be able to do so with complete accuracy based on your description of who you are and where you are headed. Although this document probably should begin with the pastor, it needs input from all the key leaders. It will be your unique bible from which everyone will draw their texts.

The document then needs to be boiled down into a two-page summary that all the leadership understands and integrates at a genetic level. It also needs a one-page version that every member can almost commit to memory. This version may become your welcome brochure or the document you give to potential donors who don't attend your church.

While there is much that could be written on this topic and others who are more qualified than I, let me offer some suggestions with regard to printed materials. Every document you produce should:

- **Be customizable.** Given the state of technology, there is no reason to give everyone the same information when people need very different information to motivate them.
- **Use color.** If you don't have the equipment with which to do this, there are businesses on every corner that can do it for you at a reasonable cost. Select your colors carefully, though. Here a professional can be very helpful. You probably don't have to hire someone, since almost

every company, institution, or large business has some-one who does this for them. Getting material designed may be a great way to get younger people involved in your ministry.

- **Use an easily readable typeface.** You are reading Palatino Linotype. Use lots of "white space" to avoid overwhelming the reader.
- **Use photographs.** Carefully select them to elicit the emotional response you desire.
- **Be proofed.** Proof it, proof it again, and then have other people proof it. You will **not** catch your own mistakes. Presenting donors with material with a mistake com-municates volumes and leads them to conclusions you'd rather avoid. You want to leave an impression of com-petency.
- **Be edited.** Edit it, edit it again, and then have someone else edit it. Eliminate all extraneous words, phrases, and descriptions. Boil it down to only the information you want to communicate. Remember white space is more likely to get people to read your information than your words are.
- **Use headlines and subheadings effectively.** That is all that half the people will read unless you catch their at-tention.
- **Never use abbreviations or insider language.** Denomi-nations are notorious for using abbreviations so much that they forget what the initials actually stand for. The United Church of Christ frequently uses the initials OCWM. It stands for "Our Church's Wider Mission."

Even the full title doesn't say anything except to true insiders. Never make a potential donor feel ignorant, uninformed, or excluded.

• • •

I once was asked to talk about the impact of a culture of fear on generosity. Certainly the events of 9/11, and the political leadership in its aftermath, had a devastating financial impact on many progressive churches. What I chose to talk about, though, was the impact of generosity on a culture of fear. This is the essence of our message. It is the point of our ministry. It is what we do and why we do it. Money is not a peripheral issue for our ministry, but, as Jesus said, our treasure is directly connected to our hearts, and to the hearts of those to whom we minister.

I'd like to appear more spiritual than I am. The truth is the motto I have lived by is not from scripture but from poet Wallace Stevens. He wrote, "After the final no there comes a yes, and on that yes the future of the world depends."

Chapter Ten
A Metanoia Church

One of my closest friends has had a very successful business career. He has risen to the top using a unique strategy. Unlike most folks who move from success to success, he has specialized in what he calls "turnarounds." He enjoys taking a failing or underperforming company and helping it to turn around and become successful.

As Christians, we ought to be the ultimate turnaround specialists. The Greek word "metanoia" occurs in the Bible dozens of times. It is generally translated "repent." Among us liberal types, the concept of repentance often has gotten a bad rap. In large part, that is because some of our fellow Christians have insisted on screaming it at us, often about things that we don't really think needed changing, like sexual orientation and progressive social values. Still, even the most liberal of us understand that the biblical concept of repentance is actually **good** news. The idea that the God who created us believes we are capable of changing the direction of our lives should encourage us and give us hope. If that is true about our lives, then why not our churches?

While *metanoia* is a multifaceted word, its basic meaning is, "To change direction." If unprofitable companies can be turned around, certainly churches or ministries that are not thriving can as well. I must confess that, on occasion, I have been asked to consult with a church that was declining and facing the end of its life and said to myself, "Saving that church is probably impossible." That is the kind of statement that can really only be made confidently by an atheist. If Easter has any meaning at all in our lives it is that God is the God of alternative endings.

So, can every situation be turned around? Our faith must say, "Yes, it is always possible." However, like humans and almost every human creation, churches have natural life cycles, and it may be that the end of a church is the natural and appropriate occurrence with the passage of time. As painful as it is, some churches must die so that something else can be born. However, I personally believe that reality should be much rarer than it is today for progressive, liberal, and mainline churches. Yes, death is the only option for some, but many simply need to find the right formula to turn around trends that, if neglected, will lead to their demise.

Turning around a loss of membership, attendance, finances, and/or vitality is never easy, and, again, this is a case of "one size fits **some**." Each situation is unique so it requires a unique solution to its challenges. However, my business friend suggests that there are basic principles and steps for any company that wants to turn around their losses, and I think that is true in our churches too. They, in fact, may be very similar. Let's see:

Ruthless Honesty

The first step may be the hardest because, for any change of direction to occur, we must be absolutely truthful about the fact that we are headed in the wrong direction. Like the old-fashioned concept of repentance, confession is a vital, though painful, stage through which we must move. If you ever have had to make a deep, soul-bearing confession of your own failures, you know just how traumatic this can be. Generally, though, our failures are not built on some major soul-rattling mistake, but are the result of a series of tiny misjudgments usually rooted in some mistaken core beliefs or self-delusion.

Every time I ask a church why they believe they are not thriving, almost everyone in the room has a quick answer. Sometimes everyone has a different theory, and sometimes it is a part of the commonly held belief of that faith community: the neighborhood is changing, population is declining, not enough parking, we lost our beloved pastor, the building is in such bad repair, etc. All of these reasons, and dozens more, certainly can contribute to the loss of vitality in a congregation, yet we all can cite examples of churches that are exceptions, churches that thrive under all of these same circumstances. The tough thing is to get below those obvious and legitimate concerns until we are able to address the root causes of a congregation's inability to be one of the exceptions.

There are a number of tools that are available to do an accurate assessment of a church's circumstances, challenges, and potential for vitality. This may be THE area where an outside "expert" may be of greatest service. Any of us can utilize the tools available, but it is difficult for a pastor or longtime lay leaders to deliver, frankly enough, the bad news that first must be ruthlessly faced. It feels like a betrayal, and it is good that the "betrayer" can go away soon after the diagnosis. Physicians often have to tell us bad news, but they generally don't have to live with us afterwards. As John Fortunato, in his book *Embracing the Exile*, puts it, "The bad news about therapy is you **don't** die." The pain of this kind of brutal honesty won't kill a church, but it can kill a relationship with a pastor who was called to preach good news, not bad.

While Elizabeth Kubler-Ross's stages of grief are no longer in vogue with counselors, they still illuminate some of the reactions our congregations have when offered a painful diagnosis. Denial is a natural first response, but it also can be a fatal one. Pretending a tumor isn't there and allowing it to grow until we are too weak to respond to treatment seems to symbolize the approach that too many non-thriving congregations take. Frankly, we pastors must accept some responsibility for being complicit in this denial. Our friends in recovery keep trying to remind us that the very definition of crazy is *doing the same thing and expecting different results*, yet I so often find myself unable to change course because I am doing what I know how to do and am terrified to admit that it is no longer working and that I need to learn some new skills.

Remembering Our Business

Closely linked to the first need required for a turnaround is the leadership answering management consultant Peter Drucker's core question: "What business are you in?" The great management guru was fond of asking that question of everyone in a company, from the board of directors to the CEO to the shipping clerk. He often noted that, while he generally would get congruent answers to the question, he almost always would get the wrong one.

"We're in the steel business," or, "We're in the hotel business." Lawyers were in the law business, and accountants in the accounting business. "No," the late Drucker said. "The purpose of the corporation is almost always to make new customers." This simple-sounding concept is at the core of Drucker's philosophy. In concert with church consultant Dr. Lyle Schaller, Drucker tried to remind us that the church is in the business of making disciples of Jesus. New disciples are our customers. Evangelism and discipleship remain the two core functions of the modern church. Reach them and teach them. The methodology we use must adapt and change almost daily, but our business remains the one assigned to us by Jesus.

Yes, building community, serving the poor, worshipping God, helping the hurting, transforming society, and confronting injustice are all quite legitimate functions of a vital church. However, these functions are carried forward by disciples. We who have devoted ourselves to the way of Jesus do the work of Jesus. There is a natural order to that, and the modern progressive church often fails to prioritize the first step. It is a great thing for a child to grow up to be a physician. However, she must first be born/come into the family; then she must be trained and educated. Even after she becomes a physician, she must be properly equipped and supported by a competent, congruent community.

Evangelism, discipleship, and service occur in that order. Churches that neglect the first two steps often find themselves giving their life for Christ without giving birth to those who will replace them after they are gone. Many of the most ancient admonitions of the Hebrew Scriptures are rooted in the

Jews' awareness that they would not survive unless they propagated. Although the rules are outdated, the principle is not. Our pews are no longer filled by our biological children, and we must borrow a page from the evangelical churches in America if we are to fill them again. How did evangelism and growth become so derided in progressive circles? If we have found our faith to be a gift, and if we believe that the values we have to offer are good, true, and transformative, we ought to be about sharing them. Evangelism is not about converting people so they won't go to hell as much as it is about liberating people from the hells in which they find themselves trapped: consumerism, purposelessness, isolation, greed, shame, fear, alienation, etc. If we have any good news for them then our first business is to offer it.

I once had to turn down a $250,000 gift. The donor wanted to endow a secular scholarship fund that the church would administer. After listening to his expectations, it was easy for me to say, "That is a great idea and a wonderfully generous thing to do, but that is not the business we are in. Let me put you in touch with someone who would be better equipped to do what you need." In the same way, after many successful years of helping people, the Cathedral of Hope had to shut down its counseling center. It was a thriving concern, but, when we looked closely at the services we were providing, we realized that what originally had been a ministry had evolved into a business. When we began the program there were few counselors to serve the lesbian and gay community, and even fewer to assist people living with AIDS. Two decades later that was no longer the case. We actually were competing with other organizations, and even businesses, to provide services that were not our specialty. The church still provides spiritual and pastoral counseling, but no longer employs 28 therapists to provide clinical psychotherapy. Like the scholarships, therapy is a very good thing; it just was not **our** thing.

It is easy to get distracted and forget what business we are in, but, as Peter Drucker observed, it also is easy to spend all of our time and resources running a machine and forget what the machine was designed to produce. All too often, I have seen churches and organizations that produce just enough resources to run the church or organization, but not enough to fulfill their purpose. That is like maintaining a machine that generates only enough energy to run the machine. No matter how beautiful or well run the machine may be, it ultimately is worthless because it serves no greater purpose than itself.

High Failure Rate

ESPN should not exist today. It does because "Sports Illustrated" forgot what business it was in. The people at "Sports Illustrated," which was launched in 1964, came to believe that they were in the business of publishing magazines. If they had remembered that their true business was providing the public with information and entertainment about sports, they would have continued to find new ways to do that. Since they did not, ESPN was born in 1979 and today has a customer base and income stream that dwarfs the magazine, which now is known as much for its swimsuit issue as its sports coverage.

Renewing the vitality of a church requires us to remember what business we are in and then to get out of our boxes in terms of how we do that business. We must dare to see new visions, dream new dreams, and try new things. The key is we must be free from our fear of failure.

While many people believe the Cathedral of Hope's growth was the result of my success rate, the truth of the matter is it was much more dependent on my failure rate. I simply tried more things that failed than most of my peers. This is a great testimony, not to me, but to the lay people with whom I had the privilege to work. The board of directors and I knew we were doing something that had never been done before; therefore, we were going to have to try a lot of things that had never been attempted before to reach our goal. We wanted to include large numbers of mostly lesbian and gay people in an institution that historically had excluded and even abused them. We also wanted to build a progressive, inclusive, and theologically-liberal congregation in one of the most conservative cities in America.

Early on, we discovered that just because someone is lesbian or gay does not mean they are progressive. In fact, as we considered the dynamics, we acknowledged that our goals would probably be met if we simply refurbished the evangelical message and ministry with which most of our "customers" had grown up. Those who grew up in more progressive faith traditions often simply walked away when they heard that, as the Methodists say, "Homosexuality is incompatible with the Christian teachings." However, those who grew up in more conservative and fear-based traditions were often the ones who clung to their faith even while acknowledging their sexual orientations. In other words, our largest market was lesbian, gay, bisexual, and transgender people who still were mostly fundamentalists or, at least, evangelicals in fear of hell. One of our church leaders observed, early on in our efforts to build a progressive church in Dallas, "This is like we are trying to build a market for a Sushi restaurant in Italy."

Trying things that didn't work was the only tool we had. We read all the books and tried repeatedly to engage various consultants. No purpose would be served by providing you the names of the churches, clergy, and consultants who refused to work with us. This rejection is one of the reasons I so love Dr. Lyle Schaller, who was unique in his willingness to help and his continued friendship. For the most part, though, we were left to find our way largely by trial and error. That can be done well only in a safe place. With very few exceptions, the congregation was willing to follow as leaders tried new things that often didn't work. My partners on the board of directors were possessed of an entrepreneurial spirit and never made me afraid that my many failures might lead them to lose confidence in me. We had some rather spectacular failures, too, but, along the way, we knew enough success to build a historically large, vital, and growing liberal church in a most unlikely setting.

I suppose I should pause to confess that, in addition to finding ways to attract record numbers of new people, I probably also hold the record for running off the most people. While many were estranged through mistakes I made, failed relationships, and my own deeply flawed humanity, a significant number left the church because we needed them to. In our more crass moments, clergy are prone to joke that our churches are just a couple of funerals away from revival, and there is more than a sliver of truth in that. When I arrived in Dallas and became clear of what the congregation's vision was for the church, I knew achieving their goals would require a redefinition of who they were as a church. They were one of the largest Metropolitan Community Churches (MCC) in the country at that time, with almost 300 members. However, that was the challenge. The congregation wanted to be a very large church: "Large enough to change the way lesbian and gay people think about God, and large enough to change how the world thinks about lesbian and gay people." Well, given that assignment, the standard MCC formula wasn't going to work, because no MCC had ever grown much beyond the size that congregation was in 1987. That remains true today.

One of the irresistible realities of life is that death is required to make way for birth. While everyone wishes it was different, there really is no escaping this truth, and no one has found a real alternative. In order for the congregation to give birth to something that had never existed before—a lesbian, gay, bisexual, and transgender megachurch—who we had been had to die. Naturally, there were those who were strongly attached to the existing values, styles, and identity. As the leadership laid out a new course, the biggest unanswered question was if people would resist changing the church they had known and loved, participate in the transformation, or simply leave. Ultimately, we discovered that those who worked for change far outnumbered those who resisted it. That is usually the case when changes are sensitively made and adequately explained. However, many churches have learned the hard way that a small group, or even a single influential resistor, can derail critically needed changes. We discovered that one of the greatest gifts we received during that time was the large number of people who simply left.

Let me say that these were not bad people. Most were folks who decided that the church they needed and wanted was different from the church we were becoming. That certainly was fair. It was a testament to the authenticity of their faith that they did not insist that the church be what they personally wanted/needed it to be but, rather, left to find a church that better met their needs. Still, the departures were painful, and a congregation already deeply in grief suffered further. As an antidote, we brought new members into the church with a great sense of joy and celebration. We expanded the ritual, had parties and celebrations, took them into the family in large groups, and encouraged them to invite family and friends to attend with them. The impression the average congregant got during that two-year span was that the church was growing rapidly. While they might have disagreed with some of the changes, they didn't question the results and were therefore much more willing to offer grace. Statistically, however, the truth was, after two years of my leadership, the church was only slightly larger than when I arrived. We had taken in many new members, but I had alienated more than a few.

If that reality had continued the results would have been disastrous. At one point another church was started in town that was made up largely of former members. This church was, and is, strongly evangelical in theology and worship and has been led by pastors who were formerly Baptist. Since Southern Baptist is, by far, the largest denomination in Dallas, it was a natural fit for the market. That church grew quickly and is today a vital and healthy congregation of around 300 members.

The formation of this church caused a great deal of fear in our leadership, but it was a wonderful gift. As our church continued to become more theologically liberal and increasingly liturgical, our sibling congregation provided a healthy and much-needed alternative. The year following their formation saw our congregation explode in growth. Although we were meeting in a wretched temporary space in an office building, we nearly doubled in size. While we grieved the loss of community with those who left, there was a liberation that we never could have anticipated. That was not because those who left were "wrong," but because we were free to answer a different call without hurting them and their needs. As painful as it was, that time was a liberating gift for us all. Although we did not see this at the time, we fortunately acted out of grace, and today we can recognize the work of the Spirit who was multiplying, not dividing.

Creating a culture of grace within the church where we can take chances and make mistakes is not optional. When a body ceases to grow and change it dies. Change always is unsettling for everyone, which is why heaping doses of grace are needed. Still, finding new ways to tell the "old, old story" is critical if we are to turn around mainline churches. What originally built our churches long ago ceased to attract crowds of new disciples and young people. We do not need to change our message so much as we must change our method. Thomas Edison always believed that his rate of success was in direct portion to the height of the trash pile outside his laboratory. He said, "I am not discouraged, because every wrong attempt discarded is another step forward." He also said, "Opportunity is missed by most people because it is dressed in overalls and looks like work."

Hard Work

I finally have reached the stage in my life where I can admit that some things didn't succeed because I simply did not want to work that hard. To be sure, one key to success for every leader is their willingness to do the work that is necessary. Much of that work must take place within us. In liberal circles "self-care" often has become the third sacrament. We have become so afraid of burning out that we never get warmed up. That may seem unkind and unfair, but I am only saying aloud what many of our lay people believe. Ministry can be a haven for the lazy, complacent, and unmotivated. Too often, we simply don't want to do the hard work that will be required to renew the vitality of the church. Over the years, I have been incredibly frustrated by a number of seminary graduates who thought they deserved to be the senior pastor of a thriving church, but were completely unwilling to earn the job or, better yet, build their own congregations. Lay people look at us and wonder how we can ask them to volunteer or take on additional responsibility in addition to the 40 or 50 hours their fulltime jobs require. Their resentment is that we are asking them to do what we seem unwilling to do. When pastors clock out after 40 hours we lose our moral right to ask our members to volunteer on their nights and weekends off.

Now, that paragraph was full of hyperbole. Many, if not most, of the clergy in this country are devoted women and men who give much more than 40 hours a week to their jobs. That is not, however, how we frequently are seen. Lay people often wonder what we do all day, and, frankly, I wonder that myself sometimes about my own day. I sure stay busy, though, and never seem to get all of my work done. Even as a borderline workaholic, I feel guilty that I am not doing enough. The secret I have discovered repeatedly, and then repeatedly forgotten, is that I have to spend my time and energy working very hard doing the right things. Doing the right things may be more important than doing things right. What is it in my weekly schedule that **only** I can do, and, ultimately, what is it that pays the biggest dividend for the church and the Realm of God?

If life was fair the things I love to spend my time doing would be the exact things that produce the most results. In case you haven't already noticed, life isn't fair. When I was a small-town Methodist pastor, I loved visiting shut-ins and people at the hospital. It is a worthwhile and fulfilling ministry, but it is not one that requires me to do it personally. During the worst of the AIDS crisis at the Cathedral of Hope it became an overwhelming and devastating ministry. I was in my mid-30s, and one day I walked into two hospital rooms, side-by-side, with four young men my age who were dying. I was almost incoherent the rest of the day. The staggering weight of that forced us to recruit large teams of people and train them for this ministry. The result was that I rarely do hospital visits anymore. The other result was that a large number of people grew as disciples and those who needed visiting received much better, and more frequent, service. At one point we had dozens of people in hospitals all over the city who were visited by the church every single day. Many times church members would be by their bedsides 24 hours a day.

I have no doubt that pastors work hard because they are devoted servants of Jesus and because they never would take money they did not earn. My challenge to most pastors is to decide where your hard work will produce the most results. Give away anything that **you** don't have to do to others. Giving away ministry doesn't give you more time to sit around and pray or watch TV or read theology or science fiction. It can free you up to invest your time and energy in places where they will have the greatest impact. Most of us are too busy now; the trouble is we too often are busy doing the wrong things.

• • •

The point is turnarounds are never easy. You have to be willing to work very hard, and your leaders do, too. You need a small group who will say, "For the next couple of years I'm willing to give this my highest priority and my best effort." You have to be willing to say that as well. It is unlikely you have an extra dozen hours a week to devote to this, so you are going to have to ruthlessly eliminate the important and do the vital. You will work harder than ever, but your focus will be doing those things that produce results — results in your own life and in the life of your church. Here, the 80/20 principle is true: 20 percent of your work will produce 80 percent of the results of your ministry. With severely limited resources, my suggestion is that pastors and congregations in turnaround situations must focus 100 percent on the productive 20 percent. Despite what I said above, you probably can't work any harder, so you must discover how to work much smarter. Take shortcuts with the important; concentrate on the vital. Let others do what others can, and you work harder on those things that will produce results:

- Vibrant worship.
- Relevant and dynamic preaching.
- Leadership training/"equipping the saints."
- Infusing disciples with the God-given vision and mission of the church.
- Evangelism: birthing the next generation.

You may have a different list, and your situation may require one. But make the list, and if it is not on the list don't do it. Then figure out how to do the list more effectively. Turning around must begin as a decision in the heart of those who are steering the ship.

Recently, I visited my parents who are quite elderly. They have been members of the First United Methodist Church in my hometown for 35 years. They both have served in almost every leadership role possible. That church was where I came to love and value strong liturgy and beautiful historic worship. That church has the most beautiful stained glass and the best organ in that part of the country. The Sunday I visited, my parents had to go to church early because they were ushering at the first service, which is held in the fellowship hall and where they sing contemporary praise songs accompanied by a band. It attracts mostly young people and college students, lasts only 45 minutes, always starts late, and sounds like organized chaos to me, yet that is where these two old Southern Methodists serve. I shook my head as they went off to church that morning, and I went to catch a plane. For a moment, I had to pause and pray that God would keep my own heart as vibrant and flexible as theirs.

That is the key to prophetic renewal for the mainline church, and it is my prayer for the heart of us all.

Chapter Eleven
Evangelism is NOT a Four-Letter Word

Vintage Churches generally do not believe that people of other faith traditions are doomed for eternity or estranged from God. The truth is we are a bit embarrassed by our evangelical friends who do. Their passion to save people from the fires of hell has sent us fleeing in the opposite direction. We would NEVER invite someone to church lest they think we are judging them. Besides, inviting someone to church is déclassé and unsophisticated, and that is a fate much worse than hell for mainline protestant churchgoers. So, evangelism has completely disappeared from almost every Vintage Church's list of ministries. For our churches to thrive, however, three things must happen in each and every one of them. How they happen is unique, but that they happen is essential. If your church is to have a future, you must have new people join you on this adventure of faith and to do that you MUST:

1. Get them to come.
2. Get them to come back.
3. Get them to stay.

In a meeting 20 years ago, someone asked what we had done to grow by 300 members in a single year. Flippantly, that is what I told them. Subsequently, I have built my consulting career on teaching churches to do those three things. Agile Church Growth System was designed entirely on helping churches to do those three simple things.

Get them to come.

In a previous generation we might have called this *evangelism*. Then, we believed that the church had something to offer that people needed. If we no longer believe that then our churches really should close. If we do believe that then we are singularly selfish people not to share what we have. What is hindering us?

Almost every person of faith believes that the community, the hope, the reconciliation, the grace, the purpose, and the meaning that we have found in our faith is a great gift. What does it say about us that we have so little passion for sharing that gift? So, call it marketing rather than evangelism if that helps, but recover the passionate belief that what we have been given by God is needed by the world and should be shared. Now that you have settled that, the question is how do you share it? How do you get them to come?

I once went to a birthday celebration that was held at a bar that is a local landmark. On Wednesday nights, they have karaoke sung to live accompaniment on an old church organ. Young people don old choir robes to sing, usually badly. Although it started slowly, I looked around at one point and then leaned over to my music director and said, "There are more people in this room than we will have at church on Sunday." It was a diverse group of young people having a great time singing and often singing along. As I have pondered that phenomenon, I wondered if our churches might not do well to advertise "Sunday Morning Karaoke." At the very least, it might reframe who we are and what we do in terms younger people understand.

That is what we must do if we are to get them to come and check us out. The first step in leading your church to grow again is getting people to visit. To do that, we have to try some new things that will change what people currently think about your church. Let me offer some specifics:

- On more than one occasion I have arrived at a church I am consulting with and gone to the front door, only to discover it covered with leaves, and dust, and, in one case, cobwebs. Regulars clearly knew to enter at the back door. However, to everyone who walk by those churches, the state of their front entrance spoke volumes. What do your front door and front yard say about your church?
- Our building looks like the conservative Southern Baptist churches of our young, urban neighborhood's grandparents. When I arrived, like most churches, coffee hour was held in the fellowship hall, which, in our case, is in the basement beneath the sanctuary. The very first Sunday I noticed that not a single visitor went down to the basement. We immediately moved coffee hour upstairs to our tiny narthex. People got their refreshments and stood on the portico and, eventually, the front plaza of the church. Even in the blaze of a Georgia summer, people stood around visiting, and guests had a hard

time escaping without someone speaking to them and inviting them back. On special occasions—and we have as many of those as we can—we serve mimosas out front. For everyone passing by, seeing a diverse congregation with lots of young people drinking out of champagne glasses shatters their image of what they thought about that building. For one thing, they now know we are alive and that we enjoy being together.

- We use the building for evangelism in other ways, too. We have a large rainbow banner that reads "God is still speaking" mounted to the building. I discovered the value of this at First Congregational Church in Montclair, NJ. Their gigantic, grey stone building was built by Wall Street barons almost 100 years ago. It was impressive back then, but what it says about the congregation today simply isn't true. This young, energetic, and inclusive congregation found the largest rainbow flag I've ever seen and attached it to their towering grey front. It said to the world, in no uncertain terms, that this church wasn't what they might have assumed. The lesbian, gay, bisexual, and transgender community in Montclair has not been the reason for that congregation's revitalization, but the colorful flag out front says to the world that this is a place where all were welcome, and it is true.

- On the front of our building, between our large white columns, we often use colorful banners to announce a sermon series. The most effective was the first year that I did a series called "Beatitudes of Broadway." It followed the assigned lectionary readings, but the special music and the modern lesson came from a Broadway musical. The banners on the front were printed in yellow and black and made to look like a Playbill. The series was such an attraction that it has become a fall staple and something for which the church is known in the community. A United Methodist Church in a bad neighborhood in Savannah, Georgia has grown from an attendance in the 20s to well more than 300 by becoming known for their theatrical productions that spill over into Sunday morning worship.

- Because our church is located in an area with a good bit of traffic, we have used corrugated plastic yard signs to announce special events, like the blessing of the animals, and other special services. We put them up for a couple of weeks, and then they disappear. We have had a number of successful special events that were advertised only on those signs. If they were left they would quickly become ineffectual, but we have discovered that, as with the banners, people pay attention because they are not always there.
- We have found that the best possible marketing of the church is our activism. A pastor in a clerical collar wearing a colorful stole at a protest or social justice action always attracts photographers and television cameras. It also says, in the clearest possible way, what your church is really like and what you value. While this is not at all the primary motive for participating in social justice actions, it is a good reason to be more conscious of your participation. Wearing T-shirts and carrying signs that identify your church is a powerful witness that there is a place of welcome for people who might hold values different from the majority. Our church participates in

Moral Mondays, the pride parade, AIDS Walk, etc. We should not take these stands anonymously, but as part of the public witness of our faith.

- Every study that has been done has shown that people first come to a church because someone invited them. All of the things listed above are primarily effective in preparing people to be invited. Now, let's be honest; the odds of the members of your church inviting their neighbors are not good. However, there are ways to increase your odds:
    - Create an atmosphere where it is expected. When something meaningful happens in worship, invite people to think about people they know who they wish had been present to experience this time of celebration, renewal, forgiveness, reconciliation, hope, peace, prayer, or whatever was meaningful that day. "The choir's music was so amazing. I can think of a number of people who I wish had been here to hear them."
    - Make the service so relevant or contemporary that when people are having "watercooler conversations" what they heard or did at church naturally comes up.
    - Encourage people to check-in on social media when they come to church. The average person has 358 friends on Facebook. If 100 people checked in at church that would mean the possibility of 35,800 people seeing your church mentioned with a personal endorsement by someone they know. That kind of advertising cannot be

bought. Perhaps you send people out at the end of every service with a question or an event they can post to Facebook or Twitter. Make sure they all "like" your church's Facebook page so that postings appear in their feed. There are hundreds of ways to use social media as tools for evangelism. Perhaps it is time to revive that team. You don't have to call it "evangelism," but a group of young people who understand social media and marketing could make inviting neighbors much more likely to happen.

Get them to come back.

So, you have increased the number of first-time visitors to your church. As I said before, the typical church averages four first-time visitors a week, or more than 200 a year. The first question to ask ruthlessly is, "Why don't those who visit come back?" Every church would do well to ask them. Of course, they will deflect the question and give only vague feedback at first, but, if you genuinely want to know, they might give you valuable information. At the very least, you will communicate to them that they really were welcomed and needed.

As I said in a previous chapter, you cannot invite someone back unless you get their contact information. Guests often will give us only their name the first time. They do that because everyone else is doing it, but they are not yet sure they want you to send them information or invite them back. Still, be certain to put their name and the date of their first visit into the database. If they do return and eventually give you their contact information, you don't want to send them a note welcoming them for the first time. Rather, you will want to send them a note that acknowledges that you know they have been there before but you are glad to be able to write and formally welcome them.

Using your database effectively will greatly increase the likelihood that those who visit will return. It may take a while, but, if you stay connected to them and send them information about events, you never know what will motivate someone to return. What we do know is that being unable to stay connected almost certainly will assure they will not return. This is increasingly a generational issue. Churches too often are managed, led, and oriented to generations that are passing and are not prepared to use technology to respond to the "young families with children" that they all say they want to attract. That generation expects you to WANT their information, look them up on social media, and respond to them accordingly if you really want them to come back.

Get them to stay.

A church of tourists is not healthy. Having people "visit" but never get engaged may make things look better on Sunday morning, but, in the end, church must be more than that one hour a week. Integration is vital for the health of the individual and the institution.

There are a myriad of ways to do this, but the bottom line is, if someone is going to make their spiritual home with you, then you must give them a friend and you must give them a job. That is you must connect them to people and you must help them find a place to serve that will change their lives.

Every church I have ever worked with has listed friendliness as only of their leading assets, and, to some degree, that is true. Almost all churches are friendly … to one another. I often have attended churches without having anyone engage me in any way other than formally. Perhaps the greatest challenge my present church has is that 80 percent of the congregation is relatively new. As a result, they still feel more like guests than hosts, so they don't tend to welcome people as well as they should because they feel like they are too new. Considering that new people attend much more irregularly today than in previous generations, it requires a much longer time for them to feel like insiders and to act like hosts. I recently asked a member who had been coming for a couple of years to show a visiting family to the nursery. They replied that they would be happy to if I would first show them where it was. That is an all too common reality I'm afraid.

No church wants to be unfriendly, but in few churches do members understand that they are hosts. A visitor who is left standing alone, reading a brochure or the bulletin board is unlikely to keep returning for long, regardless of how meaningful the worship is. This is even truer if you are a "regional" church. If you are the only church of your type in an area and someone has to drive a great distance, they are unlikely to get involved unless they very quickly make some friends. They need someone to have brunch with because their friends and neighbors live a long way away. Deliberately training people to be assertively but sensitively friendly is critical.

Giving people a job also must be a much more deliberative process. Churches make announcements or put things in the bulletin and assume that everyone knows they are needed or wanted. That is simply not true for new people. Those kinds of "y'all come" announcements are assumed to be for insiders who know the details. At the very least, set up tables at which people can get more information. Better still, have the team that is always whining that no one will help deliberately recruit new people. If someone has come to your church several times they are waiting to be asked to help, asked to come to a small group, asked to be part of the family.

• • •

Growing a church is simple but it isn't easy. Get them to come. Get them to come back. Get them to stay. Simple, right? So, why doesn't every church do it? It is hard work and requires a total reorientation for most congregations to, as I am fond of saying, take off their bibs and put on their aprons. If the church remains only, or even primarily, for our members we are a club where membership has privileges and benefits. However, if we are serious about being followers of Jesus then we must find new and creative ways to share the gifts and graces that have become ours by virtue of our faith and our faith community. If we do not then our selfishness is a sin, something else the Vintage Church doesn't talk a lot about.

A church worth saving is a church worth sharing. Let's roll up our sleeves and do both.

Epilogue
Michael's Crystal Ball

Many years ago, I was in New Orleans to consult with a church. At some point, a colleague and I were walking through Jackson Square and passed a row of women at tables where people were having their fortunes told or their palms read. As we passed, my colleague commented, "Those folks should just save their money, because if the psychics really could tell the future they would buy a lottery ticket."

Well, I make no claim to any psychic ability, except that which comes from age and observation. I also can make no claim to objectivity. I love the Vintage Church. When I was at the Cathedral of Hope, my friend and mentor, the late Lyle Schaller came to consult with us. The one thing he recommended was that we needed to offer a wide variety of worship experiences if we were to continue growing and attracting new people. We took his advice, and attempted every type of worship in every imaginable setting. Many worked for a time, but it was our traditional worship that continued to grow, so long as we continued to be innovative with it.

All of that is to say that, while the church of the future will find many different expressions, it is my conviction that the Vintage Church still has a future. After more than 40 years as a pastor, and a dozen as a consultant, here is what I predict for the future of the church and the church of the future:

We will continue to experiment with forms, but the gathered church will endure.

There will be fewer mainline churches and they will be smaller, but the traditional/Vintage Church will not die. This actually is a return to what might be considered "normal." In 1776 about 17 percent of Americans attended church. By 1876 that figure had doubled to 34 percent. What we are experiencing now is a return to those norms. The church did not die then, and it is not dying now. It is changing, but there is a great deal we can do to determine the shape of that change.

Entrepreneurial leaders will succeed, but institutional leaders will not.

For too long, seminaries have attracted compliant personalities who love the church and simply want to spend their lives there. Unfortunately, that kind of leader only will hasten the decline of congregations. In the age of megachurches, charisma and personal dynamism were most highly valued and rewarded. As we move into the future, though, the leaders who will help the church thrive, and who, therefore, will be most valued by churches, will be adaptive, agile leaders. Pastoring must become an improvisational art form. Our seminaries need to encourage and recruit the kinds of personalities that the tech industry values. Entrepreneurial leaders can reinvent church just as they have every other area of life in the past 50 years. What is still true is "everything rises and falls on leadership."

"Liberal" will stop being a four-letter word in church.

While we continue to hope that labels like "conservative," "moderate," and "liberal" will matter less, the truth is millennials believe that Christianity is a conservative institution that excludes lesbian, gay, bisexual, and transgender people; is capitalistic in economic values; demeans women (since the largest representatives of the faith don't ordain women); is racially and economically segregated; and doesn't seem to care for the environment because Jesus is coming to rapture us from earth. If Vintage Churches fail to distinguish ourselves from those values we will fail to attract a generation that overwhelmingly rejects those values. The truth is most of us do, too, but we have been too timid in communicating that.

Virginia-Highland church displays a rainbow banner outside that reads, "God is still Speaking." That banner, on a very traditional, red-brick, white-steepled building has not attracted LGBT people to the church. It has appealed mostly to couples who want their children to grow up in the kind of church that welcomes all people. Our desire to blur the lines theologically is noble, but the expression of that all too often has been our failure to distinguish who we are from the largest and most vocal expressions of the faith.

The Vintage Churches that grow will be those who have externally-focused compelling missions.

People are looking for ways to make their small amount of free time make a difference. While some want to address the root causes of injustice, most are looking for tangible ways to help the poor, the environment, the abused, and the neglected.

Churches once again can be the "charity of choice" by being the ones through whom this work gets done. A first-time visitor is looking for a place where they are needed or where they can get involved, and it won't be on the finance committee or board of trustees. They don't want to support the institution; they want a place where they and their families can make a difference in the world and, thus, a difference in their own lives. The church doesn't need to do everything, nor does it need to reinvent the wheel. By partnering with worthy organizations, new people see the church as the kind of place they want to be involved with and where they want to raise their family. As the government at every level reduces the safety net for those in need, the public will expect the church to fill the gap. If we are willing to be that kind of church, they are much more likely to come and help.

Empty nesters will return.

Most cities in America are experiencing a reverse migration. Couples who moved to the suburbs seeking better schools for their children are now returning to the cities. They MIGHT return to our empty urban churches if we invite them and give them a reason. On the other hand, suburban and rural churches are now experiencing many of the challenges that urban churches did a generation ago. Depopulation, diminished financial base, increased poverty, and homelessness all seem to be moving out from the city. The key, in whatever setting the church finds itself, is an awareness of demographic shifts.

One church I consulted with had retooled their inner-city ministry to care for the homeless and unemployed during the age of urban flight. They failed to notice that they suddenly were living again in an area with extremely high property values. The poor who they served were moving away, but they had not begun reaching out to the new empty-nesters who were moving in. For a time, these new residents did a reverse commute to their old suburban churches, but, as their lives shifted back to the city, they began looking for churches closer to their new homes. The church I was consulting with had not even considered that they might again be that church. Now they are talking about starting a soup kitchen in a nearby suburb where businesses and stores are rapidly closing and home foreclosures are soaring.

Online participation in church governance will allow us to reclaim an authentic form of congregationalism that includes more than the same people simply switching hats every year.

There will need to be some generational transitions (e.g. funerals) before this shift can be made fully, but even those who are retiring today are accustomed to virtual meetings and doing the most important business in cyberspace. Anyone 65 years of age or younger can't imagine a home without a computer any more than they can imagine one without a microwave. In order to include the oldest members of our congregations in governance and decision-making, churches still will need to make accommodations, but that will be a shift in which the remote meeting will be the norm and face-to-face meetings at the church will be the exception. Every church will need to equip a room in which those who prefer or need to meet face-to-face can come and join the majority who are meeting from home or wherever they are. We will need to explain how this allows for authentic congregational participation rather than pretending that those whose children are grown and who are retired and have time constitute the congregation.

The music and worship of the church will be preserved, but the beat and rhythm and pace will change.

Young people in my church love the "new music," by which they mean old hymns played to Latin or African rhythms. They love chants, the music of Taizé, and the repetitive choruses of contemporary Christian music used in ancient liturgical forms. They don't want music that can be sung or played or led only by professional musicians. They want to participate and be engaged. Often this does not mean singing; it may mean swaying, standing, clapping, nodding, or simply feeling the beat pass through them. The organ can play a vital role in shaping a worship experience, but it is used in new and different ways. Choirs no longer will perform anthems; they will lead the people to encounter the Holy.

The church is growing around the world, and the American church has much to learn. Music and worship are a good place to start because they will engage younger people in a church that is not an American creation. They don't believe Jesus is from Atlanta, and they want the church to stop acting as though Christianity is a white, Western invention.

Frequency of attendance in worship will continue to decline.

If we do not recognize and address what is happening we will interpret this reality as the death of interest in the church. As the generation that attended church 45 times a year shifted to a generation that attends 30 times a year, the church seemed to die by one-third, but that is not true. That was, however, the impact, and we acted as if that was what was happening. Unfortunately, that trend has not reached the bottom. New and younger members who are deeply devoted are likely to attend less than 50 percent of the time. That will result in attendance declining by another one-third, while the church remains as strong and healthy as it ever was. If we continue to measure the size of the church by Sunday morning attendance the news is going to continue to get worse as the elders who attend regularly pass. Vibrant churches will recognize this sociological trend and:

- Keep members involved in ways other than on Sunday morning: volunteer ministries, small groups, service projects, online participation.
- Utilize an effective database that tracks these new ways of being involved and recognizes and responds when someone has missed three consecutive Sundays so they know they have been missed and the pattern doesn't become permanent.
- Move to electronic automatic giving so that even when people are not physically present they are able to financially support the life and ministry of their church.
- Create events and special worship services so that throughout the year there is a large attendance other than just at Christmas and Easter.

Spiritual formation must replace Christian education.

Everyone has Google on their smartphone. If someone needs to know who the Amorites are they can look it up faster than you can remember. People will return to churches that stop trying to tell them ABOUT God and instead help them to have authentic encounters WITH God. Worship must stop being so filled with words and explanations and descriptions, and start being times of questioning, sharing, meditating, pondering, openness, mantras, awareness, etc. Churches must stop trying to teach people things that they don't really care about or need to know and take spiritual, biblical, and Christian truths and help people to integrate them into their lives. Service projects must be placed in a spiritual context, or the church becomes just another social service agency. We can't do this by expecting people to attend a class.

When Virginia-Highland Church launched a new ministry to end homelessness, the service focused on the stories in the Gospel in which Jesus was homeless. A formal litany of prayer featured pictures and descriptions of specific homeless people in our neighborhood. We didn't pray for "the homeless," but for a man named Carwash who lives under a nearby bridge. At communion, we remembered how Jesus didn't have a home to which he could bring his friends for Passover. Instead, he had to borrow an upper room. Creating these kinds of spiritual connections between our faith and current issues is much more important to millennials than knowing that several people wrote the book of Isaiah.

The Vintage Churches that survive and flourish will be the ones who find their prophetic voice.

Several years ago, I wrote a book about how the Cathedral of Hope UCC flourished as the largest lesbian, gay, bisexual, and transgender church in history even though it is located in one of the most conservative cities in America (Dallas, Texas). Many people suggested that the church grew from 280 members to more than 4,000 because it is located in the "Bible Belt." That might have been true, if there also had been LGBT megachurches in Houston, Nashville, Birmingham, and Atlanta. What was perhaps even more striking about that church than the sexual orientation of the majority of its members was that it was theologically progressive, in that setting, even liberal.

While there are a number of factors for that church's growth, I contended in my book *Prophetic Renewal* that a significant one was its willingness to claim their uniquely progressive voice. While I got a great deal of hate mail, even death threats, for claiming that LGBT people can be Christian, I got even more for opposing capital punishment in Texas and for advocating for gun control. Still, when people heard a church publically taking stands that disagreed with the majority, and with how people perceive the church in general, they came to find out there just might be a place for them. We weren't just another conservative or evangelical Texas church. The key factor, however, was that we let people know that. Driving by our church it could have been any large congregation, but, by our activism and public participation, we made clear that what distinguished us was much more than the fact that LGBT people attended. At one time, there were 37 churches in Dallas that welcomed LGBT people. The Cathedral of Hope was larger than all of them combined because we used our prophetic voice loudly to advocate not only for gay people, but for causes that were precious to lots of people, even in Texas.

The Vintage Churches that will flourish will be activist churches that can't be mistaken for communities of faith who reject the leadership of women, sanctify economic disparity, support exploiting the environment, manipulate people's fears, or believe that Jesus was a conservative American. Driving by your church, people can't tell who you are. We must repudiate our own fears of offending a few people and speak up for those without a voice so the world will know the kind of Jesus we follow.

On Sunday morning, we drive to church long before much traffic is on the road. I always take a route that I avoid most weekdays because the traffic is too heavy then, but not on Sunday mornings. Perhaps I would take it anyway. On my way from the safety and comfort of my home, to the sanctuary of my church, I always drive by the graves of Rev. Dr. Martin Luther and Coretta Scott King. I do it to remind me of the ministry to which I have been called. It isn't always easy, or comfortable, or safe, but it is important, perhaps even vital. So is yours.

• • •

I do not know whether or not your church will be one of the Vintage Churches that lives long into the 21st century. This is my last prediction, though, and I believe it with all my heart: There is going to be another Great Awakening. Millennials are deeply spiritual people who say they are "spiritual but not religious" because they see the two as mutually exclusive. What they want, and what they need, is a place where they can practice a spirituality that is life-giving, not just for themselves but for their world. YOU can be that place.

There is a fresh wind stirring in the church. Perhaps it is giving birth to new expressions, or maybe it is longing to revive vintage ones. I think it is both. What I know is that when the Spirit blows through our world in a fresh and powerful way, I want to be a part of a church that has trimmed our sails and is waiting.

So, Vintage Church, sail on, sail bravely on.

Made in the USA
Middletown, DE
02 May 2019